Life
AFTER
LOSS

Life AFTER LOSS

*A Personal Guide
Dealing with Death,
Divorce, Job Change
and Relocation*

Bob Deits

FISHER
BOOKS™

Publishers: Howard W. Fisher
         Fred W. Fisher
         Helen V. Fisher
         J. McCrary
Editors: Howard W. Fisher
         Sheryl Clapp
         J. McCrary

Published by Fisher Books
4239 W. Ina Rd., Suite 101
Tucson, Arizona 85741
520-744-6110

Notice: The information in this book is true and complete to the best of our knowledge. It is offered with no guarantees on the part of the author or Fisher Books. The author and publisher disclaim all liability in connection with use of this book.

Library of Congress Cataloging-in-Publication Data
Deits, Bob, 1933-
   Life after loss: a personal guide dealing with death, divorce, job change, and relocation / Bob Deits.
          p.   c.m.
   Includes bibliographical references and index.
   ISBN 1-55561-049-8 : $12.95
   1. Loss (Psychology)   2. Life change events.   3. Bereavement--Psychological aspects.   4. Grief.
   I. Title.
BF575.D35D45   1992
155.9'3—dc20   92-29593
                            CIP

© 1988, 1992 Fisher Books

Printed in the U.S.A.
Printing 10 9 8 7 6

Fisher Books are available at special quantity discounts for educational use. Special books, or book excerpts, can also be created to fit specific-needs. For details please write or telephone.

Contents

This book is dedicated to...

Those courageous people who shared their lives and losses with me through grief support groups.

Dr. Howard Clinebell, Jr., who taught me the deeper meanings of pastoral care.

June Deits, who has shared life with me "for better or for worse" since we were 18 years old.

Acknowledgments

I OWE SO MUCH to so many people who have helped make this book a reality that any listing is going to leave someone out. Therefore, I will first thank those whose names are not mentioned, but should have been. Thank you for your help.

I am forever grateful to Howard, Helen and Bill Fisher of Fisher Books. Somehow they saw the possibility of a useful book in the scrambled collection of words that was my original manuscript. That gratitude continues to all of their staff who had a hand in editing the subsequent versions so I could be proud of the finished product.

Mike Hammond has a special place in my heart for caring enough to introduce me to the Fishers. Thanks to my daughter, Jeanne Hughes, who told Mike of the project and urged me to follow-up on our initial meeting with Howard and Bill.

More than 30 very busy people took time to read early versions of the manuscript. I thank all of them for providing valuable insights that are reflected in the book.

The Staff-Parish Relations Committee and congregation at St. Paul's United Methodist Church allowed me time out from my pastoral and administrative duties to write. My fellow clergy on our staff filled in for me many times. I thank all of you.

A special thanks goes to my brother, Frank Deits, whose genius with computers is exceeded only by the patience he showed in teaching me how to use one. I *never* would have made it without him! Thanks, too, to Frank's wife, Mary Deits, a professional counselor, for sharing her special understanding of the relationship between the body and emotions.

I'm grateful to all the pioneers in the field of understanding grief and loss, but especially to Dr. Glen Davidson, Rabbi Earl Grollman, D.D., Dr. Elisabeth Kübler-Ross, Rabbi Harold Kushner, Dr. Howard Clinebell, Jr. and Dr. Granger Westburg. These people have made a great contribution to human happiness by breaking the silence barrier and making grief something that can be talked about openly.

I am grateful most of all to my loving wife and best friend, June. She insisted I had something to say that needs to be heard, urged me to write it, made sacrifices too numerous to mention so I had time to write, proof and read every word dozens of times and would not let me quit until the book was finished.

Bob Deits

Introduction

THIS BOOK IS ABOUT the kinds of losses we all experience. It is a book for *doing* as much as it is for reading. It is about life, loss, grief and, most importantly, it is about life after loss. In the pages that follow, you will find help in coping with major losses in your own life and resources for enabling you to help others with their losses.

If you haven't experienced a major loss recently, you undoubtedly know someone who has. And you need to know that such losses are an inevitable part of everyone's life at some time—and yes, there are things you can do to prepare for facing major losses in your life.

Have you lost someone who was an important part of your life? Perhaps your spouse, your child, a parent or other close family member has died. Or it could be a good friend, a co-worker or neighbor.

There are other losses, all of which confront us with an extraordinary amount of emotional pain: divorce, the loss of a job, physical disability, relocating from one place to another, traumatic injury, limitations due to aging (such as no longer being able to drive a car or loss of mental capacity), personal bankruptcy or business failure.

If you are female and even suspect that you may have been sexually molested as a child, you are one of an extraordinarily large number of women who have experienced the trauma of this major loss. If you are male, the numbers are a little smaller, but the sense of loss is just as painful and the grief process just as difficult as it is for women.

For many people, the death of a pet is a particularly difficult experience.

After reading this book, you will have a better idea of what to expect of yourself and others when life collapses in tragedy. You will know the difference between normal and distorted grief responses. You will recognize behavior that seems crazy as being a healthy sign of your healing, and know the warning signs that say it's time for professional help. You will know how to care for your physical well-being while making your way along the path to grief recovery.

This is a book you will turn to many times. Loss is a fact of being alive in a mortal, imperfect world.

No one is immune from loss. Rabbi Harold Kushner was absolutely correct—bad things do happen to good people. Major loss is a fact of life for the good, the not-so-good and everyone in between. Likewise, having one major loss does not prevent you from having other losses. *Life After Loss* will help you cope with a present loss and be better prepared for those in the future.

Loss is painful beyond words. No one can anticipate the emotional and spiritual agony a major loss brings. Life can seem to lose its meaning. You may find your sense of self-worth diminished. The sadness and loneliness you feel may seem to consume all your energy. The best news is: You won't always feel as you do during the first months after a major loss. The best support is a group of other people who have also experienced loss and grief. *Life After Loss* will tell you how to find or form a grief support group and what to do during the first several sessions.

Grief that is out of control can destroy your happiness and your health. Your chances of developing a serious illness can be many times higher than normal after a major loss — but it doesn't have to be that way. You can strengthen your own immune system and help your moods be more positive. There are other definite things you can do to protect your health while you work to recover your happiness. You will find these things spelled out in detail throughout this book. They have worked for thousands of others and they can work for you too.

Death is not the only loss that calls for grieving. We expect to grieve when a loved one dies. But it is equally as important to mourn the death of a relationship when a divorce occurs, the loss of familiar surroundings when relocating to another city, the loss of a job or any other loss that makes a major impact on the quality of our happiness. All the risk factors that follow a death also apply to any other major loss.

You can have a satisfying and meaningful life after any loss. The worst of losses is not the end of life for you. The life stories of countless numbers of people who have made it through is your guarantee. Grief is always about losing, but you can also find growth. You can take charge of your journey through grief just as others have done by following the steps given in this book.

Grief doesn't have to be a passive thing. It isn't something that happens *to* you. Grieving is first and foremost something *you do* to heal your wounds after experiencing a terrible loss in your life.

The longer I have been with people in their losses, the more convinced I have become that grief can be turned into something positive. There is much more to do in response to a major loss than just wait and suffer.

The many exercises you will find throughout the book will teach you how to do everything from getting a good night's sleep, to helping yourself cry, to learning the power of keeping a daily journal and how to ask for help, to saying good-bye to some part of your personal history that is now past.

Life After Loss will help you recognize responses to major losses that often seem bizarre but which are perfectly normal. For instance, to be forgetful is not to lose your mind, to be angry at a deceased loved one is not wrong and tears are the best of all signs that you are doing fine!

You will also learn a puzzling and valuable truth: While grief is an intensely personal experience, working your way through grief effectively isn't done alone.

Many years of being involved in other people's losses have shown me that grief is not ugly. Neither is it an illness. Grief recovery is more like recovering your balance after being knocked from your feet than getting over a cold or the flu.

This book contains personal accounts of many people's responses to a variety of loss experiences — including my own. I hope that as you read you will become less anxious about your own losses, and better prepared to handle future losses in your life. To do these things is to develop grief "fitness."

One of the great discoveries you will make is that your very best friend in times of grief and loss is *you!* You are the one person who can turn the pain of your loss into a creative hurt.

The subject of God and our losses is always an emotional and delicate one. I do not attempt to offer you an explanation of why God allows your loved ones to die, your dreams to be shattered or why you must suffer.

Instead, you will find help in this book for dealing with the spiritual dimension of grief as with every other aspect of loss. Used appropriately, religion can be an important tool for grief recovery. If abused, it can be an almost insurmountable barrier to healing.

I wrote the first edition of *Life After Loss* because I was convinced that loss and grief are not our enemies, but that living in constant fear of them is. The effectiveness it has had in helping thousands of people find a full and rewarding life after the worst of losses has served to deepen my conviction. This revised edition contains more stories of real-life people and the new insights they have given me about how all of us can get very good at doing grief.

Perhaps the greatest benefit of this book continues to be not what it can do to bring comfort to your life after loss, but what it will do to bring quality to your life *before* a major loss.

Loss and the Mourning After

Loss is a fact of being alive

THERE IS NO EXPERIENCE more common than losing someone or something of vital importance to you. When this happens, there is no response more normal or appropriate than grief. Loss and the grief that goes with it may well be the number-one proof that you are flesh and blood, a real, live human being.

Every day the news is filled with accounts of death, divorce and business failure. AIDS spreads like a plague. The want ads testify to the fact that the average family moves once every five years, losing close association with their friends, family and familiar surroundings. Our minds cannot begin to comprehend the numbers of children who are molested or sexually abused in some way, leaving emotional scars that last a lifetime.

Amazingly, all of these common loss experiences are buried in a conspiracy of silence. With rare exceptions, nobody wants to talk about loss.

We pretend loss only happens to people who deserve to be punished. If pushed, we will admit that nobody lives forever, but we are quick to say that death always happens some other time than now. We are especially sure that major loss is something that happens to others.

Jim had a heart attack (actually three attacks within a few hours) while at work. His symptoms were classic and clear—a racing heart beat, pain and pressure in the chest, cold sweat and nausea. He fought off weakness and dizziness while climbing three flights of stairs—all the time telling himself that heart attacks did not happen to him. In looking back after the attack, he could see he had been denying the early signs for months. Jim is no different from the rest of us.

Ask yourself these questions:

❖ *Do I understand that my spouse, child, mother and father, or my dearest friend could die at any moment?*

❖ *How would I handle the divorce I thought could never happen to me?*

❖ *If a routine physical examination revealed cancer, how would I react?*

❖ *How would my sense of personal value be affected if I lost my job?*

❖ *How would I feel if I sold the home I have lived in for years and moved to a strange new city?*

The better you can handle loss in your life, the healthier and happier you will be. This begins with facing loss as a normal part of life and being willing to talk about it.

That's the purpose of this book, to offer you a new and deeper understanding of the large and small losses in your life and help you express the many feelings you will have about those losses. It also recommends how to work your way through those losses and protect your mental and physical health during the process.

Every major loss makes a dramatic impact on your life. These losses continue to influence all areas of your life for a much longer period of time than you may realize. In addition to the obvious emotional and physical effects of a major loss, you may find your performance at work is diminished, your spirituality may not be as satisfying, you may experience sleep disturbance and you may have a significant weight gain or loss.

It is not uncommon to have a current loss "call up" some prior loss from many years earlier. Thinking about these losses is not enjoyable, but it is necessary.

You will have more losses. That, too, is a fact of life. Your family and friends will also have losses. Loss is an inescapable part of being alive. It may not seem fair, but it is real.

❖ *Every marriage ends in one of two ways: death or divorce.*

❖ *Every human relationship is temporary.*

❖ *Every career has an end.*

❖ *Not every goal you have in life will be achieved.*

❖ *The aging process is inevitable and so are the losses that come with it.*

The good news is that you can get through a major loss experience and not be destroyed by it.

Scotty had crippling arthritis for most of her adult life. For many years before her death, she was confined to a wheelchair. Her hands were so twisted she had to be fed by someone else. Pain was her constant adversary. Nevertheless, Scotty was always a vivacious person with a winning smile, a sharp wit and an unbeatable will to get the very most out of life she could.

Scotty shed plenty of tears. She knew what it was to lose physical skills most of us take for granted. Sometimes her disease robbed her of her dignity. She acknowledged her loss of physical strength and wellness. She refused to allow it to destroy her spirit or make her bitter. Until the very end, she remained a fully alive person who was an inspiration for those who knew her.

Most of us look for happiness and fulfillment in our achievements. We measure success by how much we gain in life. Because of this, our joy can be wiped out at any time by *one* major loss.

Jim and Jo had planned their retirement for years. They budgeted carefully; he was diligent in his work and they were successful with their investments. When the day of Jim's retirement arrived it was a dream come true. The long-awaited motorhome was parked in their driveway— waiting for its first adventure on the open road. Two months later, Jim died of a massive heart attack.

For Randy it was a different kind of loss. He was a career-oriented person who let nothing get in the way of his rise to the top of the corporate ladder. He worked long hours and earned lots of money.

When his wife complained that they had no social or intimate life together, he reminded her that she should be grateful for their beautiful home and expensive cars. There would be time for fun and games later. One day a man arrived at Randy's office to present him with divorce papers. When I met with Randy he was trying to adjust to living in an apartment, seeing his children only on a court-appointed schedule and learning to be single again at the age of 38.

Ed and Rena faced yet another kind of major loss. Ed

had received a fine job promotion complete with a sizable increase in pay. However, the new job required them to move from the midwestern city in which they had lived all their lives to a desert community in Arizona. Rena and Ed's joy at their good fortune lasted about a month. Then, their sense of loss set in.

They missed their old house, friends, family, church and familiar surroundings. Rena even missed the climate she had looked forward to leaving. They could not seem to enjoy their new environment. No church seemed to measure up to the one they left behind. The people in their neighborhood seemed cold and unfriendly. In less than six months Rena and Ed had packed up their belongings to go back to the old job (at the old salary), the old neighborhood, old church and the old weather.

But when they arrived "home," things weren't the same. They did not enjoy the climate. Their dream of a new life was lost. Their sense of self-esteem was diminished. They felt they had failed.

And consider Dorothy and Cecil who recently celebrated their sixtieth wedding anniversary. The problem is that Cecil has had Alzheimer's disease for several years. He is confined to a rest home where he is aware only of being cold or hungry. He hasn't recognized his wife for some time and the cost of his care is extremely high. Dorothy tries to carry on a style and grace that brings the admiration of everyone. She has a quick wit and a compassion for others that now has her caring for a sister who is terminally ill with cancer. But the tears are always poised just below the surface and she struggles from time to time with the agonizing question "why?"

The word that describes what is happening to Dorothy is "grief." It's the same word that describes the experiences of Scotty, Jo, Randy, Ed and Rena. It also describes your experience and mine. You will experience grief with *every* loss.

"Grief" is the perfect word to describe a normal response to the loss of a parent, spouse, child, pet, job, marriage, stage of life, healthy body or mind, familiar environment, self-respect, love affair or any other loss experience you can name.

Because it is inevitable, it is important to know that "grief" is not a bad word! Neither is it a sign of weakness or a lack of religious faith. Grief isn't something you should try to avoid at all costs and "get over" as quickly as possible. It isn't better to feel joy than to feel grief. It is certainly more *fun* to feel joy—but it isn't better. The best thing to feel is whatever is appropriate to the events of your life. If something good or pleasant is happening, it is appropriate to be *joyful*. If you have experienced loss, it is equally appropriate to be *sad*.

If you have had a major loss, you know that well-meaning friends will reward you for hiding your grief in their presence. If you can keep from crying in public, even after the worst loss experience of your life, someone is going to praise you for doing so "well."

The problem is, *not* crying is totally inappropriate behavior and can put you at great risk of physical and emotional disease. When anyone wants you to hold the expression of your grief in check, remember, what they are seeking is *their* comfort, not your welfare. To really do well, you must express your sadness freely for as long as it takes to release it.

Many polls and studies have asked the public, "How long should it take to mourn the death of a loved one?" The most common answer was we should be finished grieving between 48 hours and two weeks after the death! In truth, we aren't even started in that length of time.

Research by Dr. Glen Davidson of Southern Illinois University, a pioneer in researching the bereavement process, revealed it takes most people at least two years to begin returning to a normal life after a major loss.[1]

There is even danger in establishing two years as a reasonable length of time to finish mourning. Yogi Berra, the colorful former major-league baseball player and manager, once said that a game "isn't over until it's over."

That's the way it is with the grief process after a major loss. It's finished when it's finished. I often hear someone say, "I am so relieved to know that others still don't have everything worked out! I thought I was the only one who wasn't handling my loss as I should."

There's very little that is reasonable about grief. There is nothing sensible or reasonable about losing someone we love. There is nothing easy about seeing our marriage end. There is nothing rational about any major loss. Whatever the loss, it is a devastating experience. The last thing any of us needs at such a time is a load of guilt because we aren't responding in the "right" way!

If you are having problems with a loss after two, three or four years, there is a reason: You aren't finished with your grief. That doesn't mean you are weak. It doesn't make you a bad person. It just means you have more work to do. You don't need to feel embarrassed or shy about seeking help in doing it.

Although the fact the grieving process takes so long is surprising, it is not negative or morbid. Remember, the presence of grief means your loss was significant to you. The sadness and emptiness you feel are appropriate responses.

Earl Grollman, internationally known counselor on death and dying, has said the loss of a loved one is the most stressful of *all* of life's changes. "You may look into the mirror and not even recognize the way you now look. Something in you is gone which can never be regained."[2]

Your grief is a symbol of the quality of the relationship you had with the person who has died. Rather than trying to hide your grief, I encourage you to wear the signs of it as an Olympic gold medal. Your tears, the heaviness of your heart and the overwhelming sense of loneliness all say, "This person, this marriage, this part of my life has been so important to me that nothing will ever be the same again. My grief is the last act of love I have to give. I will wear it with pride."

Remember that not everything is bad in a marriage that ends in divorce. In the worst of marriages there are times shared that are good and meaningful. These, too, are worth your grief. If nothing else, your shattered dreams are worthy of your tears.

The mere fact that you are divorced can itself be a terrible loss. Nancy said to me, "I think I grieved over the fact that I was now a divorcee. It was a label I never wanted to have."

Neither is there anything wrong with acknowledging the significance of our roots in a familiar place by grieving the loss of that place when we move away.

Even less-significant losses in your life will hang around in the recesses of your memory and emotions, gathering energy until they have enough combined force to make themselves felt.

Have you ever found yourself overreacting to some disappointment? Do you have times when you are irritable and short-tempered without knowing why? Such behavior often results from having some relatively minor loss experience call forth the gathered energy of several buried losses from the past.

The desert community in which I live often experiences a gathering of thunderhead clouds on summer afternoons. Sometimes the result is little more than higher humidity and soft breezes. On other occasions the breezes become a dirt-scouring wind followed by intense rain. Local weathermen tell us these monsoons happen when the atmosphere has stored up the right conditions and something serves as the trigger to turn it loose.

Our accumulation of loss experiences is like that. We

store them up over a period of time until something happens that triggers the outpouring of all our pent-up feelings. It should be no surprise that we sometimes cry our eyes out over a seemingly minor disappointment.

Norman Cousins said, "Death is not the enemy. Living in constant fear of it is." I would paraphrase that to say: Loss is not the enemy. Living in constant fear of it is.

Because of books such as this one, the lid is off of the subject of grief and loss. It is no longer taboo to say you are grieving. If we begin accepting grief as a normal response to loss, it becomes something we are free to feel without seeing ourselves as weak. If we understand it isn't a forbidden subject, we can lay any sense of guilt aside and break the silence about our experience. To do these things is to take the first steps toward discovering a full and rewarding life after any loss.

[1] Glen W. Davidson. *Understanding Mourning.* Minneapolis: Augsburg, 1984.

[2] Earl Grollman. *Time Remembered.* Boston: Beacon Press, 1987.

2

When the
Bad News Comes

First responses to a major loss

I WAS SITTING IN A CONFERENCE with about 500 other people. There was a large chalkboard at the front on which messages for the participants were written. I saw the messenger go to the board, but paid little attention to the message until I realized it was my name that had been spelled out. When I reached the telephone, someone told me my mother was dead. To this day I can't remember who called to break the bad news.

Mom was only 54. Although I knew her history of health problems, I never suspected she would die so young. She had just begun a new treatment and was responding well. No one considered her illness to be life-threatening. While I was at the conference, she simply went to bed one night and died in her sleep of arteriosclerotic heart disease.

I turned away from the telephone in that state of hazy confusion I have seen so often in others after a major loss. I didn't know what to do or where to turn. At that moment our minister appeared and I muttered in a dull flat voice, "my mother died." One day less than six months later I found my father's body in his apartment where it had lain for 24 hours. He too died of a heart attack. He was 57.

Responding to Death

What do you do when they say the word "dead"? The first thing you do if you're like most of us is go into a state of shock. After that you are apt to do just about anything. The first seven days are often a blur about which little is remembered later.

There really isn't anything you can plan to do in the first few hours and days after news of a shocking loss. You can't anticipate how you will react to the death of someone dear to you. Even if you have had other losses, each experience is different and you may react in quite different ways.

I am amazed at the number of people I meet at funerals who are over 60 and have never before lost a loved one to death. If your experience is death-free, it becomes doubly important that you not wait until a death occurs before talking about it.

Husbands and wives do each other a big favor by talking about the almost certainty that they will not die at the same time. That conversation should start soon after the wedding if not before. It's a sobering thought for engaged couples to hear that every marriage ends in either divorce or death, but that's a fact. It isn't fun to talk about death, but neither is it depressing or morbid unless we make it that way.

The best thing I can tell you about first hearing the bad news is that whatever your reaction is, it will be normal and okay. Some people pass out, others are icy calm. Some fall apart in tears, others become the world's greatest organizers.

No reaction is better or worse than any other. It doesn't mean you cared less if you don't become hysterical. You aren't weaker if you cry or more courageous if you don't.

In the long run, tears are a good thing and an encouraging sign. A good rule of thumb is: If you haven't "let it all out" by the time three months have passed, you probably should seek counseling.

However, you know yourself better than anyone else knows you. If you aren't given to tears in other settings, you may not be at a time of loss. If you don't feel like crying in the first few hours or days, don't worry about it! If after some time you feel like crying but can't, seek professional help.

Caring for Yourself after
the Death of a Loved One

When you experience any major loss you need to take special care of yourself. Here are seven actions you can take to help you through this very difficult time:

1. Assess your state of health before your loss. If you have been under a doctor's care recently, or if you have any history of heart problems, strokes, high blood pressure or any other serious health problem, get in touch with your doctor *now*.

2. Be very careful about what you eat and drink. Food may be of very little interest to you. Nevertheless, you will

need all the energy and emotional strength you can muster. Going long periods of time without eating, then consuming foods with little or no nutritional value, or drinking large quantities of beverages with caffeine or alcohol is not good. See Appendix B for nutrition guidelines.

3. Talk about the deceased person. Talk with anyone and everyone who will listen to you. Reminisce about past good times and tell stories that are unique to the one who has died. Do not hesitate to talk about the events surrounding the death. You may find yourself telling the story of how the death occurred over and over again. That's normal and good.

4. Make time for solitude. Sometime before the funeral be alone with yourself. Allow yourself flexibility of time, but a minimum of an hour. Say to yourself out loud: "_____ is dead; he or she is dead." Don't say *gone* or *passed away* or *passed on*. Use the word *dead*. You need to hear yourself say it. Don't be afraid of your emotions. Not even hysteria will hurt you.

5. Go to bed as close to your normal bedtime as possible. Do this even if you don't feel like sleeping. It is important to keep your normal routine intact as much as possible. Avoid tranquilizing yourself with medication, drugs or alcohol.

6. Allow your support community to help you. This may be your church, synagogue, friends at work, members of a lodge, a club or any other group of people outside your family.

Many people won't know what to say, but that doesn't matter. It is their presence that counts. Tell that to whomever comes to give you support.

You may find that prayer and other religious practices do not come easily. That, too, is normal. In the first hours, you may even forget the name of your rabbi, priest or minister. Again, don't worry about it. Your faith will catch up with you along the way.

7. Allow yourself to have angry feelings. If you find yourself angry at the world in general and at God in particular, allow yourself to feel those emotions. It won't hurt the world, God or you! Remember: Even though you know the answers, it is always okay to ask "why?"

Getting Through the Funeral

The funeral usually takes place three to five days after a death. However, delays sometimes occur due to the cause of death, distance family members have to travel, weather and availability of a facility and someone to officiate. But three to five days is typical under normal circumstances.

Your time will be taken up with decisions that often only you can make. If you are responsible for making arrangements, you have to:

❖ *Select a mortuary.*

❖ *Make decisions about the date and time of the funeral.*

❖ *Decide whether the casket will be open or closed.*

❖ *Decide whether or not to have a memorial service without the casket present.*

❖ *Make arrangements for the body to be buried in an earthen grave or above-ground crypt.*

❖ *Choose embalment or cremation. If cremation is chosen, decide if the cremains are to be buried, placed in a niche or scattered.*

❖ *Select someone to officiate at the funeral. In most cases that will be a priest, rabbi or minister.*

❖ *Make seemingly endless phone calls, each of which is just as hard to make as the one before it.*

❖ *Locate insurance papers, birth certificates and military records, if any.*

❖ *In some circumstances, decide if there is to be an autopsy.*

❖ *Arrange for copies of the death certificate.*

You will probably not want to do any of this. But it must be done. Actually, it is a kind of strange blessing in disguise. Friends of the deceased or other relatives who have no demands made upon them often have a rougher time in the first few days than those who have all the responsibility. Making funeral arrangements and doing all the other necessary tasks is a release for many people. It is something concrete and real to be done at a time when everything else seems so unreal.

It is good to seek the assistance of someone who is a step removed from the shock. This could be a neighbor, friend, clergy (we do it all the time) or counselor. Ask this person to go with you to the mortuary, help select a casket and assemble clothing for the funeral, if needed. If you must drive a car during the first few days, be very careful. You will be easily distracted and your reaction time may be considerably slower than normal.

It isn't fair that you should have to make decisions that can have such long-lasting effects (such as the cost of the funeral) when you are in a poor mental condition to make them. But the pressure to make a disposition of the body and do something about a funeral doesn't wait until you feel better. For these reasons a trusted outsider can be a tremendous help.

The funeral director can also help with many details and offer good counsel. I have heard stories about unscrupulous morticians who take advantage of people in a time of crisis, but in more than 20 years of being involved in funerals, I have never encountered such a case. The funeral directors I know are honest business people who have a genuine concern for those who come to them.

The Day of the Funeral

The day of the funeral is unlike any other day you have lived. If you are a family member, you are the center of attention. You may think you are in a giant fish bowl and the whole world is watching you suffer. The only good thing that happens at the time of a loved one's death is that your extended family gathers for a reunion. Telling stories, recalling the past and giving each other support can infuse you with a special measure of strength.

Many religious communities bring food for the family on the day of the funeral. This relieves the pressure on you to take care of feeding people after the funeral. If anybody offers to provide food, take them up on it. Suggest the number of dessert items be limited. Neither you nor your family needs a "sugar fix" during this time of extreme stress. Excessive sugar often gives you a boost for an hour or two, but it is followed by a rapid drop in energy and mood.

Drugs and Tranquilizers

Don't take tranquilizers, drugs or alcohol before the funeral. The service is designed to help you more than it is to do anything for the deceased.

To get the most help from the funeral you need to:

❖ *Be as aware as possible of what is happening.*

❖ *Be in touch with your feelings.*

❖ *Be expressing your grief.*

The funeral is often the first time the death becomes real for you. As painful as this is, experiencing the reality of your loss at the funeral can be quite important to you a few weeks or months down the road.

Neither you nor anyone in your family needs to be strong for each other or for friends and community. This is not the time to play *Marvelous Christian*, *Noble Jew* or *Super Trooper*. It is not your job to show how well you can care for everyone else.

Viewing the Body

One decision that just about everybody faces is whether or not to view the body of the deceased before or at the funeral.

There is one hard and fast rule about viewing the body: *Do whatever you feel like doing or not doing.* There is no right or wrong way to do it.

Many people find that viewing the body prior to the service helps them bring closure on the reality of the death. Seeing the body of your loved one in a casket makes it difficult for you to run and hide from your loss.

It isn't wrong to touch the body. When my wife's brother was killed, she was not able to accept the reality of his death and begin mourning until we went to the funeral home and she touched him. If you have never touched a dead body, it helps relieve the initial shock if you know that the body will feel very cold to you and the skin has a more leathery texture.

If your loved one was ill for a long time before death, perhaps confined to a hospital intensive care unit with all the tubes and machines hooked up, you may find relief and comfort in seeing the person look more peaceful.

You can also choose a private family viewing before anyone else arrives to allow time to get over the initial shock and be more in control in public.

On the other hand, you may want to remember the

person as you last saw him or her. It may be that the circumstances surrounding the death make it impossible or undesirable for you to view the body. If you have heart problems or high blood pressure it may be desirable for you to deal with the loss more slowly.

Whatever you decide is perfectly okay as long as it is not a way of denying the death. You will do enough of that in a few days anyway. If you are in doubt about what to do, can't decide and are in good physical health, I suggest you view the body in private, then decide what you want to do at the funeral.

Responding to Divorce

The death of a family member is not the only loss that triggers grief and mourning. What do you do when the word is "divorce"? The shock of that announcement is no less than that of a death.

Let's suppose you have been reasonably happy in your marriage. It has not been all peaches and cream, but then, whose is? One day, out of the blue, your spouse announces that he or she wants a divorce.

Or, you have been unhappy in your marriage relationship for several years. Perhaps you have "hung in there" because of the children, or maybe you hoped that one day things would be different. Now it has become intolerable to go on with the charade. You have gathered up your courage. Tonight you will tell your spouse that you want a divorce.

Whether you are the one who initiates the divorce or the one who is shocked by the decision of your spouse, both situations represent a major loss.

If either of those situations fits you, you need to know that a number of other questions usually surface when a divorce is imminent. You may wonder:

❖ *Am I doing the right thing?*

❖ *How can this be happening to me?*

❖ *What will our friends think?*

❖ *How can I face my family?*

The shock that follows the realization that divorce is inevitable is like the shock that follows the news of the death of someone dear to us.

In the case of divorce, it is not a person who has died, but a relationship and dreams from your wedding day. For all of the divorces that happen in our society, I have not performed a wedding yet where the bride and groom expected anything less than a lifetime of marriage.

Acknowledging that your marriage has failed is very much like hearing that your spouse is dead. Some divorced persons have told me they think it is even worse!

Sally spoke for many when she said, "If my husband were dead I would at least have a body to bury and something I could do. This way he is still walking around and I have only my pride to bury. If I were a widow I would get sympathy from our friends. As a divorcee I get blamed for it!"

Caring for Yourself after Divorce

The first seven days after the announcement of a divorce is also a time when you would do well to take special care of yourself. I recommend you take the following steps:

1. Assess your own state of health prior to your divorce or separation. Yes, this is the same as the first step after a death! If you are under a doctor's care, or if you have any history of heart problems or high blood pressure, get in touch with your doctor right away.

2. Be careful of what you eat and drink. Yes, this is the

same, too. You may want to respond to your anger and emotional upheaval by going on a food or alcohol binge. The desire is understandable, but the results are not helpful.

3. Find someone with whom you can talk freely. What you need more than anything right now is an understanding ear. Find a person who will listen without making judgments or offering too much advice, someone who genuinely cares about you. As in the case of a death, it is important to talk about how it happened. Did you make the decision? Or did your spouse drop the bomb on you? What feelings do you have? Talking is crucial!

4. Don't keep your divorce secret. Let your family, friends, clergy, fellow employees and business associates know of your situation as soon as possible. The fear of other people's rejection is almost always worse than reality.

The sooner you can be open about what is happening the better. You have nothing to be ashamed of. If family members, friends or clergy don't understand, they have a greater problem than you do.

5. Don't give your immediate feelings long-lasting importance. If you are like most divorcing people, your emotions will run the gamut between anger and panic. If you were the one to make the decision to file for divorce, you may go through a period of sheer euphoria. If you had no idea that a breakup was coming, you may feel betrayed and crushed.

Try to remember that you won't always feel as you do now. If you are high, you will probably have a sudden drop somewhere along the way. If you are torn apart, you will recover.

6. Seek legal advice and emotional/spiritual help. Get both before you make decisions that can't be changed. I can't begin to tell you the amount of unnecessary grief I

have seen people bring themselves because they acted on their own volatile emotions instead of seeking legal counsel.

Likewise, everyone I have known who has come out of a divorce truly on top of life has benefited from good psychological and spiritual counseling. Where children are involved, this is an absolute must.

Responding to Other Losses

What do you do when they say the word "fired"? Or the words cancer, amputation, moving, early retirement, bankruptcy, senility, failure, or any word that identifies a loss of self-esteem, love, familiar surroundings or security?

There is no doubt that some losses will affect you more than others, but all losses do affect you.

Your loss experiences are like pages in a journal about your life. When a new page is added, the story of all your losses is told again.

Whenever you experience loss of any kind, doing the following will help get you on the right track through your grief:

1. Identify precisely what it is you have lost. For instance, in a bankruptcy the loss of money or income is often not as traumatic as the loss of self-esteem.

Make a list of the loss or losses. There are usually more than one in any loss experience that you sense. Identify the feelings you have about each by using the list of feeling words in Appendix A. Which loss calls forth the strongest feelings? That's the place to begin.

2. Do a personal assessment. What is your physical, emotional, intellectual and spiritual condition right now?

These dimensions of your personhood do not exist in isolation from each other. Your attitude affects your emotions, your emotions affect you physically, your physical condition affects both your emotions and attitude. And your spiritual outlook affects everything else.

Where do you need help? Identify the best source of help for you in that area. You might need counseling or just a vacation. Follow up on seeking whatever help you need.

3. Talk about your loss and your grief. Tell anyone who will listen to you about your loss. Tell as many people as you can. Don't be hesitant to call your reaction by its correct name: *grief*.

Keep a journal of who you have talked to about your loss and the date you talked with them.

Set a goal for yourself to tell at least one or two people about your loss every day for the first week.

4. Find a support community. You need people who will be with you for the duration of your grief, whether that is a few days or several years.

If you belong to a church or synagogue, you have a ready-made source of people. Your religious community either has an existing support group or has a need for one. You can be sure there are other people waiting for someone like you to call a group together.

If you are not part of a religious community, you can find a church or synagogue that has such a group, or look for people in your neighborhood, service club or workplace. If you are unable to locate an existing support group, you may have to create one.

Loss and grief are universal human experiences. You can be sure there are many others around you who need the support as much as you do. Reaching out is often a very difficult thing to do when you are struggling with grief. But you will be rewarded with a strong network of support that makes the pathway through grief easier.

The Deafening Sound of Silence

For some days following the death of a loved one, you will be surrounded by caring family members and friends. But the day comes all too soon when family members must return to their own lives and friends seem to weary of trying to cope with your grief.

If you are divorcing, friends and family will rally to your side and be ready to listen to your complaints and comfort your tears—for a few days. Then they will go back to their own lives and expect you to get on with yours.

Two weeks after her husband's death, Marjorie said, "One day you are the center of attention and it seems everybody cares about you and shares your loss. You wake up the next day and everybody is gone. You are more alone than you have ever been in your entire life. It is so quiet that the silence is deafening."

The shock of Marjorie's loss had worn off at about the same time her support system went home.

Those of us in churches and synagogues have failed people by pouring out compassion and care for about a week when someone dies—and then disappearing like fog before the rising sun. Being with people through the funeral is good. But it is after the funeral that the real work of grief recovery begins—and lasts for three years or more.

Preparing for the Weeks to Come

After any major loss, you may have a very difficult time reaching out for help. People will tell you to call them whenever you need them. At the moment you need them the most, the thought of calling may never cross your mind! You will feel lonely and confused. You will wish that somebody would come along to do something without your having to ask.

Most of the time, no one will come. It doesn't mean no one cares. It simply reflects the truth that not many people understand loss and grief. It is time for you to begin taking charge. Write the following information on a note pad and put it by your telephone:

1. Name and telephone number of your minister, priest or rabbi.

If you haven't had regular contact with a clergyperson, use the one who officiated at the funeral. If that isn't feasible, think of the emotionally strongest and most understanding person you know. Put that person's name on the pad.

In the case of divorce do the same. Ask yourself who has been divorced and seemed to grow through the experience.

Test the reliability of this source of help by calling that person *before* you really need them. Ask if you can call during the night in a crisis. Remember, a "no" answer doesn't mean you are rejected. It means that the other person is either over-stressed, is not able to cope with grief or has some other perfectly valid reason for being unable to offer you that availability.

I have about two-thousand people to look after in my congregation. There is no way I can always be available to everybody. I am fortunate to have three associates and a group of specially trained lay persons to help carry the load. But there are still times when I have to say "no" to someone. If your first choice can't help you, call another person. Once you have connected with someone who is available, be sure you:

❖ *Never call at an inconvenient hour unless it is a crisis time for you, and…*

❖ *Never hesitate to call when you do have a need.*

2. Name and telephone numbers of your doctor, in-

cluding the after-hours number and address and tele-phone number of the nearest hospital.

3. Names and telephone numbers of the family mem-bers with whom you can talk the most freely.

These should be the ones you would want notified in the case of any emergency.

Writing down this information and keeping it by your telephone gives you the security of not having to remem-ber names or telephone numbers in an emergency or when you are distraught. It is also a way of beginning to take charge of your life again.

If you are employed, go back to work as soon as you can. But be sure to have a conference with your supervi-sor, a business associate, or whomever needs to know that for the next few weeks or months you may not function as efficiently as you did before. Assure them your perform-ance will return to normal—and believe yourself that it will.

You may find that a day is going along reasonably smoothly when something calls you back to the intensity of your loss and grief, and you will need to go home or take a break until you can regain your composure.

It is not uncommon to think you see your deceased loved one in a crowd or hear them in another room. An ad on radio or television can call back some poignant memory. So can a song or the conversation of fellow employees. These kinds of events can trigger a barrage of tears. Those with whom you work need to know that it doesn't mean you are falling apart, but it is just a sign of your process of recovery.

Going home to an empty house can be terrifying. So can waiting for your husband to pull into the driveway at his regular time and suddenly remembering that he isn't coming home—now or ever.

Mothers who have lost young children to death often

have a bad time at the hour of their child's nap or bath, or when other children are coming home from school.

You may find it difficult to go out of the house. Facing the world again as a widowed or divorced person is a strange sensation.

One widow had not driven a car for 10 years before her husband's death. When he died, she had to learn again. Not only was it frightening to face traffic, but each time she got behind the wheel she was reminded that she was there only because her husband was dead. For several months she found her grief intensified each time she drove.

The divorcing person has most of the same things to face as the widowed person, plus some others. Widowed people get sympathy at least in the early going, but few will seem to care how much your divorce is hurting.

The divorced husband typically has to relocate, usually to an apartment. Housekeeping, meals and laundry can be real problems. People seem to expect that every male who gets divorced is overjoyed at gaining his "freedom" and can hardly wait to start playing around. Actually, most of the men I talk with are scared to death of the prospect of entering the dating scene again. And, their grief at the loss of their children can be intense.

Women with young children have the awesome task of becoming single parents and trying to meet the needs of their youngsters without much help. Most of the time a divorce is costly enough that the family home must be sold, both persons must work and childcare must be arranged. The standard of living declines dramatically.

Like everyone else who experiences grief, you will have to face some things for which you are not ready. Some-times, you will think you are the only one to have ever felt like you are feeling right now. You may think you are losing your mind and going crazy. You may wish that you could run away or die. You will feel as lonely as you have felt in your entire life.

Hear this message: You are normal! What is happening is to be expected. It is a necessary step through grief. It must be faced. It will pass. You will conquer this thing.

3

Recovering
Your Balance

Getting back on your feet

THE GRIEF YOU EXPERIENCE after a major loss will require a time of recovery. It may take much longer than you anticipate to feel "normal" again. But this doesn't mean your grief is an illness. Recovering from your loss is not like recovering from the flu. It doesn't help to take two aspirin, go to bed and wait for grief to go away.

I have been with people who tried to medicate their way through grief. It doesn't work, but I'll admit it's tempting. And it usually isn't difficult to find a doctor who is willing to prescribe tranquilizers for the first few days or weeks. Being medicated often does more harm than good. It can cloud the awareness of your feelings, cause confusion and inhibit the progress of grief recovery.

The only time medication is called for is in the case of *extreme* depression or anxiety. I would understand that to mean the person is totally dysfunctional. In those instances, the combination of carefully prescribed medication and psychotherapy can be necessary as an emergency intervention. Such times are quite rare in my experience with bereaved persons.

To take control of your grief, you must face your loss head-on with all your senses working. You can't do that while you are blissfully tranquilized.

Grief recovery is more like recovering your balance after being knocked off your feet. When you suffer a major loss such as a death in the family, divorce or relocation, it feels as if you have been run over by a very large truck. It affects you emotionally, physically and spiritually. You are disoriented, shocked, uncertain and devastated. You may feel so tired that even thinking requires a tremendous effort. Your faith system may be as shattered as your life seems to be.

Before you can pick up the pieces and go on with any sense of purpose and fulfillment, you need to regain a sense of balance.

After the death of a loved one, people often tell me, "I am crushed" or "It knocked me flat." These are not overstatements. They are good descriptions of what we experience. Life seems to fall apart. We can become disoriented and have memory lapses. I am frequently told how difficult it is for people to go back to work or to church.

Other family relationships are often affected in dramatic ways:

❖ *A divorce can result in confused loyalties among family members.*

❖ *After the death of one child, you may struggle with
   your feelings about your other children.*

❖ *The death of your spouse can make it seem as if no
   other family member really matters — or cares.*

Linda and her husband had gone for a walk at sunset.
They talked about the things they would do when he
retired, although that was still more than 10 years away.
Early the next morning she awoke to the sound of his
gasping for breath. He died an hour after reaching the
hospital without ever regaining consciousness.

Linda described her reaction to his death, "I felt as if a
quick-freeze tube had been run down my throat and my
heart and emotions were frozen. I didn't cry until the
funeral was over. I didn't feel any particular sadness at first.
I didn't really feel anything at all. I was like a zombie going
through the motions of living. But inside, I was as dead as
my husband."

Other people respond with hysteria. Mary was driving
a group of neighborhood children to the ice-cream store.
Somewhere along the way, her own toddler choked to
death in the back seat. She didn't know anything was
wrong until they arrived at their destination.

On the day of the funeral the family called me to say
Mary was hyperventilating. As soon as she could breathe
again, she would scream hysterically until her breath was
once more gone. I went to the house and ordered everyone out of the room, except for Mary.

When we were alone, I told her that I was there to be
with her, that I understood both the immensity of her loss
and her sense of guilt. I said, "Mary, you can respond any
way you want to this terrible thing. It's okay with me if you
hyperventilate, scream, throw-up, wet your pants — anything that will help you get through the funeral this afternoon. I won't let you be harmed, and there are plenty of

folks here to help clean up any messes."

She looked at me squarely in the eyes for a long time, and then threw her arms around my neck, sobbing not in hysteria, but in anguish that was totally appropriate to the loss of her baby.

Later, she could not remember being out of control, only that she felt better after my arrival.

It isn't better to remain calm or to fall apart in tears. There was nothing wrong with the way either Mary or Linda reacted to their losses. Each responded in ways that helped protect her shattered emotions. Without being aware of it, they were beginning to recover.

In the first few days or weeks after a loss, it isn't even better to be gracious rather than bitter. Your initial reaction will be involuntary—like a sneeze if something tickles your nose. It's a good time to remember that you won't always feel as you do at the moment.

You will react to a major loss in your life in ways you can't predict. You will have been knocked off-center. It will seem as if the foundation blocks of your life have crumbled. You should expect it will take time for you to recover your sense of balance.

Try thinking back to some loss in your life:

❖ *Remember how your life crumbled under that experience.*

❖ *Write down some of the feelings you had at that time. See Appendix A for a list of words to help you describe your feelings.*

❖ *With whom did you talk about those feelings?*

If you are like most of us, you kept much of what you were thinking and feeling to yourself.

Grief and loss are experiences we have not talked about nearly enough. Because of this conspiracy of

silence, we often make our task of recovering more difficult. We often think there is something wrong with a
perfectly normal reaction.

"You mean other people do that? I thought I was going
crazy!" That's the single most frequent thing I hear from
people in grief support groups. The truth is very few
people experience mental illness during grief recovery,
but almost everyone does crazy things. When a loved one
has died (or even your pet), you may struggle with issues
of security, self-esteem and depression. You will do and
think things that seem strange to you and, perhaps, to
others.

Forgetfulness

During the first three or four months after a major loss it
is very normal to become forgetful. Widows tell me to
encourage newly widowed people to keep an extra set of
car keys in one of those magnetic boxes placed under a
fender of their car. They recommend having a trusted
neighbor keep an extra set of house keys. Even the most
well-known telephone numbers should be written down
with copies placed near the phone and kept on your
person.

This advice to widowed persons applies equally to
parents who have lost a child and those who are going
through a divorce. When we moved to a new state, I locked
my keys in the car four times during the first six months
we were there. It happens to all of us.

You may find that you have forgotten how to do the
tasks that have been most routine for you. Sue was a
secretary who regularly typed 80 words per minute with
flawless accuracy. A month after her divorce she complained she could not type her own name correctly. When
my grandmother had to give up living alone and move in

with us, she forgot that our coffee pot was electric and put it on the stove burner. By the time the odor of burning plastic reached us, it was destroyed.

Whenever I meet with a group of bereaved persons, some time is inevitably spent laughing at ourselves for our forgetfulness. What's happening is the emotional equivalent to overloading an electrical circuit. When our minds and emotions have had too much stress, they seem to "short-out." That isn't a bad thing. I see it as a protective mechanism that is an automatic reflex. It's a necessary step for most of us that allows our emotional resources to gain strength for the difficult task of grief recovery.

You will continue to recover your sense of balance. The experiences you have during the early weeks and months are part of the process. The more you understand that what is happening to you is normal, the less the process will frighten you. There is comfort in knowing that others behave in the same ways.

The following exercise has been well tested by people all across the country. It can help you take the first step in recovering your balance.

Write this on a piece of paper. Make at least three copies:

❖ *I will not always feel as I do now.*

❖ *I am doing okay. Grief will not hurt me.*

❖ *I will make it through my loss as others have made it through theirs.*

Post one copy on the door of your refrigerator. Put another somewhere in your bathroom—preferably on the mirror. (You will use these household items regardless of your grief!) Keep the third copy in your purse or wallet.

Every time you see these statements, read them aloud. Keep reading them until you know them by heart and the words come automatically in moments of special sadness.

Being forgetful is like the sadness, fatigue, anger and other parts of your grief experience. They are signs of your movement along the pathway to recovery. You aren't falling apart. You are coming together.

You won't always feel like this. You can recover your balance and your life.

The Pattern of Recovery

Recovering your balance after a major loss will tend to follow a fairly predictable pattern. But it may seem like the pattern of a crazy quilt. You need to know this. It isn't as if you can ride an escalator from the basement of grief to the penthouse of joy. Neither is it like climbing a set of stairs with a firm tread and good, solid handrail.

If you are like most of us, you will have times when your recovery feels like a hopeless maze with no way out. Sometimes, the signs of your progress will seem to be signs of regression. About the time you think you have some part of your grief figured out, something new rises to challenge you.

The best image I can think of to describe the pathway of recovery is to picture yourself trying to walk the greased tracks of a roller coaster—in a rainstorm. It's frightening. You feel terribly uncertain. You take three steps forward and slip back two. There is a strong fear of falling and being unable to get up. It feels "messy" and uncomfortable.

But in the end you will make it. You will reach your destination. You will know you have achieved a significant victory. Life will be whole again.

Tears

Along the way of your journey to wholeness, you will shed more tears than you thought your body could hold. Four months after her husband's death, a widow said, "I now understand why they say the human body is mostly water. I've cried enough tears to fill a swimming pool!"

I am a big believer in tears. There is a sign on my office wall that reads, "People and Tears are Welcome Here." I always keep a full box of tissues in plain sight and several more in the closet. When someone comes in to talk about the breakup of a marriage or the death of a spouse, or a child who has run away, I want that person to feel free to cry as much as needed.

If you have had a major loss within the last three months to a year, you ought to be crying. If anything, that's more true if you are a man than it is if you are a woman. Most males have grown up with the command, "Big boys don't cry!" That's one of the unhealthiest bits of information anyone could have given.

Crying is one of the healthiest things you can do. Studies have shown that tears of sadness have a different chemical makeup than tears of joy. Tears of sadness release substances that have a calming effect. It is no myth that you feel better after a good cry. Tears are also one of the signs that you are beginning the process of recovery.

Jack came to see me a few months after his wife died. He had been absent from church since her death. In the past, the two of them rarely missed a Sunday. He told me he had reached the church door several times, but just couldn't come in. He would begin to cry as the memories rushed over him of having Helen beside him and listening to her sing the hymns. Each time he tried to come in he would turn around at the door and go home to cry alone. He didn't want anyone to see him "being weak."

As we talked, I discovered that he wasn't sleeping well and was eating infrequently. He was also having occasional chest pains and shortness of breath.

I told Jack that his unwillingness to cry was hurting him and blocking his ability to handle Helen's loss. It might sound unkind, but I scolded him for allowing his pride to keep him away from church and his lack of confidence in the rest of us being able to handle his grief.

I told him our church Cry Room at the back of the sanctuary was not only for parents with babies, but for adults who needed to cry and were uncomfortable doing it in public. I also urged him to join the grief support group where he could talk and cry with other folks who would understand. Jack took me up on both suggestions.

Within a matter of weeks he was out of the Cry Room and back among the congregation. He began to sleep better and eat better. In time, his physical health returned to normal.

Like Jack, you will be able to handle your losses and grief better if you have some idea of what to expect of yourself. It helps to know that:

❖ *Tears are a sign of healing, not weakness.*

❖ *You are not alone in your feelings.*

❖ *Grief will take a while.*

❖ *You will move through various stages of recovery.*

❖ *There are visible signs of your progress.*

Any loss is upsetting. It isn't just a death that upsets your sense of balance. It is important to remember that divorce, moving, financial loss, children leaving home and illness are among many other experiences that can also have devastating effects on you.

These kinds of experiences happen to everyone. They knock you off balance. You must recover that balance before life can go on. That recovery takes time and attention and work.

If you don't take the time to pay attention to your grief and do the work, life after a major loss will never again be as full as it could be.

4

Steps to Recovery

Walking the path to wholeness

RECOVERING FROM A MAJOR LOSS is one of the most difficult challenges any of us faces. Your life will seem shattered into a million pieces and you will be challenged to make it whole again. It is like taking a forced journey along a path that seems to twist and turn while confronting you with endless hurdles to overcome. To complete the journey successfully requires more perseverance than anything else.

Exactly how any of us experiences grief will vary as widely as our personalities and life histories. However, there are certain steps along the path to recovered wholeness that you can expect to take. Some of these steps will seem automatic—out of your control. Others will require enormous will power. They will cover a span of time that varies from a few weeks to three years or more.

Understanding these steps to wholeness will help you deal with your grief more effectively. You will know that you are making progress, even when it feels as if you are slipping backwards. You will not have the added burden of thinking there is something wrong with you when you are reacting in a perfectly normal manner.

You will also be able to help family and friends understand more of what is happening to you and how they can best give their support.

The steps are:

❖ *Shock and numbness*

❖ *Denial and withdrawal*

❖ *Acknowledgment and pain*

❖ *Adapting and renewal*

Shock and Numbness

In the first seven to ten days after a major loss you will probably feel stunned, shocked and overwhelmed. You may feel "frozen" or hysterical. In any case, you will have a difficult time later remembering much of what took place.

Your reaction is a result of a reflex action that shuts down your entire emotional system. Whatever your initial outward reaction, you will have a certain numbness inside. I like to think of it as God or nature providing a temporary cushion against the full impact of our losses. It's a brief stop at a resting place before we begin the long journey through the agony of grief to a renewed sense of joy.

A few days after the death of a loved one, when the funeral is over and relatives have gone home, the shock begins to wear off. This is a good time to have someone with you. It is a poor time to make any decisions that will have a lasting impact on your life.

People who give away clothing and possessions, decide to move from their homes or quit jobs within a few weeks of a loved one's death often regret those decisions.

In the case of divorce, the shock comes either with the announcement by one spouse to the other of the desire for a divorce, or the actual filing.

I answered the phone one day to hear the familiar voice of Jim, a dear friend of many years. He was calling from another state. His voice was hushed as he said, "Bob, Marge wants a divorce. She doesn't want to be married to me anymore! I keep saying this can't be happening to us, that I'll wake up any minute—I can't believe it!"

Now it was my turn to be shocked. We had known Jim and Marge for more than 12 years. We had shared many family experiences together. I thought I knew these people as well as anyone in my own family. They were the last couple I would have expected to divorce.

I mumbled something to Jim about telling me what happened, but I can't remember what he said after that. My mind was racing back over the long hours we had spent at a mountain cabin talking about our future plans—the mythical restaurant we had planned in the greatest detail; the trips we would take; sharing our children's weddings. None of this would happen now. Tears welled up in my eyes.

When I hung up the telephone, I sat at my desk in silence for several minutes, maybe a half hour or more. I really don't know. My tears flowed more freely as the words, "Oh, no," repeated themselves over and over in my mind.

Finally, it occurred to me that I had to call my wife to tell her. When she answered, I could barely get the words out. I'm sure I went on with my work that day, but I am equally sure I was only going through the motions.

The shock of losing our friends as a married couple was magnified by the loss of the dream we had for the future. I found I could not approach this divorce with any sense of professional detachment.

For Jim and Marge, the shock came in facing the reality of their lost dreams. Children loved by both had to live in separate homes. There was property to be divided. Friends and family had to be told. It wasn't the way they had planned their lives! There were also the unavoidable sense of failure, the rejection, the anger and all the harsh words.

Jim and Marge taught me that the shock and grief that comes with divorce is not less than that which comes with death. It takes the same week or so for the shock to wear off. And it takes a lengthy time to complete the recovery.

The shock we encounter as we move to a new city comes when we first confront the strangeness of our new environment. A young couple, carrying a small baby, came to my office one day in tears. They had arrived in town a few days before. Everything had seemed okay. They had a place to live. He was to start his new work assignment on Monday. Their belongings had arrived undamaged.

But, on that particular morning the baby had awakened with a fever. All of a sudden the shock hit. They didn't know where to begin looking for a doctor in this large city. They had come from a town with one percent of our population. Back home they knew the doctor, the druggist, the postman and the mayor on a first-name basis. This wasn't home and they felt lost.

Shock will follow every loss experience to some degree. You may have been "cool and collected" as you prepared for surgery—and found yourself "coming unglued" as they came to take you to the operating room. The realization that "it" is really going to happen can be a shock to the strongest of us.

Shock can last from a few hours to several days, depending upon the severity of your loss. The important things for you to know are that:

❖ *It is a necessary first step to recovery.*

❖ *It won't last long.*

❖ *It's not a time for long-term decision making.*

❖ *It's good to have a trusted friend with you.*

❖ *When the shock leaves the pain comes.*

Denial and Withdrawal

When the shock wears off, you may not be ready to face the reality of your loss. You will want to deny the thing that has happened with all your strength.

No one can begin to describe the incredible depth of pain you may feel when a loved one dies. If you have already had that experience, you understand. If you haven't lost someone to death, think about some other personal loss you have had. The death of a pet can be a very painful loss. People grieve over lost friendships, the move from familiar places and bitter disappointments.

You will probably not want to face those deeper experiences. We seldom stop to think that *our* parents, spouses or children are going to die someday—and the loss of these important people *can* be within our own lifetime.

No one plans on a divorce at the time of marriage. When we think about relocating, we are usually more aware of new places to be seen than old ones to be lost.

We aren't ready for loss as a part of life. Therefore, when it happens to us, we try to deny it. After an initial reaction of "Oh, no!" most of our denial happens below the level of awareness.

Some of the signs of denial and withdrawal you can expect to see in yourself are:

❖ *Feeling weak and drained of energy*

❖ *Lack of appetite*

❖ *Lack of sleep or oversleeping*

❖ *A frequent dry mouth*

❖ *Physical aches and pains*

❖ *Lack of concern with personal hygiene or grooming*

❖ *Fantasies of the deceased or divorced person*

❖ *Expecting a dead or divorced person to come back*

❖ *Disillusionment with your new city or home*

❖ *Anger*

❖ *Inability to perform routine tasks*

All of these are normal reactions to loss. You may experience one or several of them at a time. It's quite possible you will think you are over some reaction and weeks or even months later it will return.

If you know denial and withdrawal are to be expected after a loss, you can say to yourself, "This reaction is normal. This is another step on the way through grief. I will not always feel like this." I have seen many people recover energy for the task of grieving simply from saying words like these.

This is a time when problems with family and friends may surface. If your closest friends and members of your immediate family don't respond to your grief in ways that are helpful, you aren't alone. Even those who know you best will not understand your grief any better than you do.

Well-meaning people who really care about you will want you to "be okay" much more quickly than you can be. Most won't know what to say to you. Some will avoid you.

At the same time, you may find that you are too fatigued to reach out for help. Even making a telephone call can seem like an insurmountable task. You will want others to reach out to you, but you will not be able to tell them what to do or say to help. You will want to tell the story of your loss again and again. The world around you will be through listening long before you are through with the need to talk. Some will "reward" you with kind words and more frequent visits if you pretend to be on top of things. It won't seem to matter that you feel like you are dying inside.

If you understand that these conflicts are normal, you can be more patient with others—and with yourself.

This is especially helpful when anger surges up within you and you want to blame *somebody* for your loss.

Linda came into our grief support group two months after the death of her husband. She was filled with anger, blaming everyone for his death, including herself. In one exercise she wrote the following to herself:

Dear Linda,

Did you do all you possibly could to help Earl? Do you believe everything a doctor says? Don't you know that most doctors are in it for the money and not to help people? They took the easy way out with Earl. All they wanted was their thirty pieces of silver!

Linda, don't you think you should have noticed Earl's health more? Instead of going for a walk with him you could have taken him to a heart specialist. You say you didn't know anything was wrong. Why not? If you had been a little more observant my partner Death and I would not have paid you a visit.

Sincerely,
Grief

The anger and blame in Linda's letter may be unreasonable, but there is very little reasonable about grief at this point in the journey to recovery. Read the letter again and picture some hurtful loss of your own as you do. Change the names and circumstances to fit your experience. See if Linda didn't express feelings and anguish that you have also felt. Know that these kinds of reactions are signs of your denial of the loss. They are a symbol of your mind's effort to withdraw from the pain. It isn't wrong to do this. It may even be necessary for your survival in the early months after a major loss.

It is important to recognize the signs of denial and understand them as a part of your grief. It's a difficult step of recovery because you are least able to reach out when you most need to do so. Others are least able to help at the time you most need help. The more you know about what to expect, the less isolated and helpless you will feel.

Acknowledgment and Pain

The classic psychologist calls this *acceptance and pain*. I do not refer to this step as *acceptance* because of Ann. She joined our grief support group after her husband choked to death in his sleep. I was talking about accepting our losses one day when Ann broke in to say, "Bob, the word *acceptance* carries with it some sense of approval and there is no way I will ever approve of my husband's death. I'm ready to *acknowledge* that he is dead and he isn't coming back, but I refuse to accept or approve it!" Every person in every group I have talked with since agrees with Ann.

Acknowledging your loss is the most important step of your recovery. It is at this point that you will again take full charge of your life and full responsibility for your feelings. A noticeable sense of balance is coming back into your life when you can acknowledge that your loss is real—and permanent. It represents a giant step toward full recovery.

However, acknowledging your loss can cause you extreme emotional pain. For that reason, it is not at all unusual to find yourself stepping back into periods of denial and withdrawal.

If you have had a loss through death or divorce, you will probably be ready to acknowledge your loss fully in about three to six months. However, if it takes a year or more, you won't be the first. Nor will it mean you aren't doing as well as someone else.

When Rae joined our grief support group, it had been 18 months since her husband's death. When asked why she had decided to come at this point in time, she replied, "I thought I was doing fine. I handled the funeral okay and went to work shortly afterward. I was lonely at times, especially in the evenings. But all in all I thought I was doing pretty good. In the last month, it's as if I'm right back at the beginning. I didn't cry the first time around, but now I cry all the time."

Rae had not been ready to acknowledge her husband's death "the first time around." Now she was. It was important for Rae to see she was not going backward, but forward, because she was crying now. She wasn't worse than she had been for 18 months, she was better. She was ready to move on. In the months that followed she did just that.

If you have never had a major loss in your life, you may not be able to understand the depth of pain that acknowledging such a loss can bring. My wife June has had major surgery. I never have. I can remain naïve about the meaning of surgical pain and the sense of loss that goes with it. June cannot. For her to face surgery now would be something quite different than it would be for me.

Grief is like that. When I first started meeting with a group of widows, I had to say to them, "You are the experts here. I am an amateur. My parents have died, my brother-in-law died at age six, I have moved to a strange city and all my children have left home. These losses I can understand. But, I don't know what it feels like to have my spouse die, and furthermore, I don't want to know! You will have to tell me about that experience and I will try to understand."

As you acknowledge your own loss, it will help if you remember that others can't experience the pain you are feeling. They don't know how difficult it is for you to face the reality of whatever has happened to you.

There is nothing easy about saying "I am divorced" or "My child is dead" or "This part of my life is over." It hurts! But, it won't hurt forever. Emotional pain is another of the signs of progress towards a full life. It is important at this point of your recovery to remind yourself often that you will not always feel as you do at the moment.

It will be tempting to return to a time of denial. You can do that and you will feel better—for a little while. But the only pathway to balance and wholeness lies through the pain of acknowledgment. This is when a support group or professional counseling can be of great help. People around you will ask, "How are you?" The expected answer is "fine," regardless of how you are actually feeling. If you aren't fine and you tell the truth, you will be ignored by many people as if you hadn't said a thing.

A counselor or a support group can provide a place where you can talk freely and know that others understand. There is little else you need as much right now. Because this step takes so long, it is extremely important that you have a strong support system along the way.

You will not stay immersed in agony for a year and then wake up one morning to be finished with it. The pathway to grief recovery is never a smooth one, but it does have its ups as well as its downs. Those who have been there assure the rest of us that slowly, but surely, the good days begin to outnumber the bad ones.

Adapting and Renewal

The first sign that the roughest part of your grief is over is a change in the questions you are asking. From the time of your loss the most haunting and persistent question is, "Why did this happen to me?" The day will come, often a year or more after the loss, when a new question will emerge. That question is, "How can I grow through this tragic event to become a better person?"

When you stop asking "why?" and begin asking "how?" you are beginning to adapt to your new life without the person, place or condition that has been lost.

"Why?" Questions

The worst thing about "why?" questions is there are no satisfactory answers to them. Questions that begin with "why" reflect your desperate yearning for meaning and purpose in your loss. It seems so unfair. You are sure there is some reason for it to happen. You think you might feel better and hurt less if you could just discover that reason.

Lois' son was playing golf when he was struck by lightning and killed instantly. There were four young men standing together when the fatal bolt struck. Her son just happened to be the tallest of the group. For months the one question that dominated Lois' mind was, "Why Derek? He was happily married, had a great job with a great future. Why was it him?"

❖ *Why did my husband die when he was such a good man and others who don't care about their families live?*

❖ *Why did my wife want someone else when I've provided so well for her?*

❖ *Why did we have to move to this godforsaken place?*

"How?" Questions

Questions that begin with "how" indicate you are ready to face the reality of your loss. They also express your search for ways to put together a life after the loss.

Pauline's mother died in May. A year later her son died in the same month. Two years later her husband also died in May. When she came to the grief support group more than a year after his death, she said, "I had to wait until I was finished asking 'why?' before I could come. I reached a point where I had to move on with my life or die. I have come here to find out how I can keep going."

These questions include such things as:

❖ *How can I fill the void in my life that my wife's death has left?*

❖ *How do I learn from my divorce so I won't make the same mistakes again?*

❖ *How can we make friends in our new city so we will feel more at home?*

It is difficult for us to accept that some things, even tragic deaths, happen for no purpose. It's easier to forget the word "accident" means just that—something that happens because this is not a perfect world with a perfect script written for life.

When your questions begin to change from "why?" to "how?" you are accepting that accidents include your tragic loss, too.

I want you to be able to say with confidence:

The loss I experienced is a major event in my life. Perhaps it is the worst thing that will ever happen to me. But it is not the end of my life. I can still have a full and rewarding life. Grief has taught me much, and I will use it to be a better person than before my loss.

This is never an easy thing to say. It isn't easy to think those things after a major loss. It is more difficult to say the words aloud. It can't be rushed. But it is a reasonable and reachable goal.

When you can say those things about your loss, you will find a renewed energy and enthusiasm for life. You will begin to adapt to a new life that will not revolve around your loss experience and grief. You will have a new sense of self-worth. If you are like most people, you will find a new calmness within yourself. Little things won't irritate you as much. You will take yourself less seriously and you will laugh more.

This is a good time to obey an urge to have a new hairstyle or wardrobe—or both! It may be a good time to redecorate a room or take a trip. It's time to establish new goals for yourself over the next two to five years.

As time goes on you will realize that your recovery is a lifelong process of adapting to other changes and losses. As it is with any skill, you will get better and better as you continue using the new resources you have learned from this loss. You won't forget your loss. It will always be a part of your life history. But, you will be able to think about the person, the place or whatever was lost to you without pain.

The day will come when you will know deep inside that you have recovered your balance, completed your journey through grief and are ready to get on with a good and full life. On that day, you will be a stronger person than you have ever been before.

Healthy vs. Distorted Grief

Grief is the nuclear energy of our emotions. Understood, respected, harnessed and directed, it can be a creative force. However, when grief is out of control, distorted and misunderstood, it can become a destructive force. As with other wounds, grief wounds can become infected.

It is important, therefore, to recognize when your grief is healthy and when it is distorted. If you have a common cold, you know how to care for it. You don't need a doctor or a hospital. But if your cold becomes pneumonia, it would be foolish not to seek professional help.

The same thing is true about grief. As you read through the steps to recovery that I have described, I hope you found your fears diminishing. I hope you learned more about what to expect of yourself as you experience healthy grief. However, I also want you to know some of the signs of distorted grief.

Here is a list of symptoms that indicate you have had all the stress you can handle alone. The presence of any of these symptoms says it is time to call in professional help. Remember—there is no shame in seeking help. The only shame would be if you needed help and did not get it.

1. Persistent thoughts of self-destruction—The key word is *persistent*. It is not unusual to have suicidal thoughts during grief, but they should pass quickly. If you begin thinking of a specific method and occasion for taking your life, it is time to seek help. The key decision for healthy grief is, *"I will live."*

2. Failure to provide for basic needs—If you find yourself changing your patterns of activity and avoiding friends and family, it is time to seek help. Interaction with other people is essential to healthy grief.

Equally important is paying attention to your physical needs including nutrition, fluids, exercise and rest. If you are failing to take care of these fundamental needs, it is time to seek help.

3. Persistence of one particular reaction to grief—Depression that immobilizes you for weeks is a sign professional help is needed. So is continued denial of the reality of your loss or finding yourself still without feelings months later. Help is needed when any normal grief reactions persist too long.

4. Substance abuse — This means everything from using tranquilizers or sleeping pills for too long to engaging in alcohol or drug abuse. It also includes eating too much, too little or surviving on junk food.

5. Mental illness — Persistent feelings of anxiety, hallucinations or a collapse of body functions indicates emotional breakdown. A good rule of thumb: Anytime you are unable to function normally, seek professional help.

If you are in doubt about seeking psychological help — do it! Your minister, priest or rabbi can probably refer you to someone who specializes in grief counseling. When making contact with a counselor, don't be hesitant to ask if he or she has experience working with grief. You will know within one or two sessions whether the person will be helpful to you. If you do not sense a good understanding of your grief process, try another counselor.

Even if your grief is normal and healthy, you can use all the resources you can get to help you recover your balance and put life together again.

5

The Inward
Search

Grief is a very personal experience

T O RECOVER YOUR BALANCE after loss and go on with
a happy and healthy life, you will need to search within
yourself for understanding and hope. No one else can give
you the answers to the questions that burn in your heart
and mind.

Your loss is first and foremost *yours,* regardless of who
else is affected. Because loss is so personal, it is often very
difficult to share your feelings with others and equally
difficult for them to understand you. The loneliness you
feel magnifies your sense of pain and isolation.

Your recovery is also a personal experience. How you
respond to your loss will be similar to the way your friends
and family handle their losses. But it will also be uniquely

yours because you are a unique person.

If your spouse dies, you will be concerned about other family members. You may worry about the welfare of your children after a divorce. You may care about the impact of a business failure on other investors. But your first concern and the thing that will dominate your feelings is your sense of *personal* loss.

You will not ask, "Why has this happened to *us?*" You will ask "Why has this happened to *me?*" Others can give you help and encouragement, but *you* must take charge of your grief and your recovery. It is up to you to decide if your loss will be an occasion for growth in addition to being a time of grief.

In the months that follow any significant loss, the words you will use most frequently are *I, my*, and *me*. Not only is it okay to use these self-centered words, it's necessary.

Think of a loss you experienced sometime in the past. If that loss was severe enough, it became the center of your life experience. As far as you were concerned it didn't matter if the sun was shining brightly. To you the days were dark and gloomy. It did no good for some well-meaning person to try to cheer you up with reminders of all the reasons you had to be thankful. Your loved one was gone, that place called *home* was far away or your dream was shattered. You were in no mood for platitudes.

In your heart it was pouring rain—and the sadness was about to leak out of your eyes. The orders you gave yourself to calm down didn't work. You had lost something or someone very important to you. That loss hurt beyond words.

The thing you wanted more than anything else was some glimmer of hope. You wanted to know if there was a light at the end of the misery tunnel. If there was such a light, you wanted to know it was not an oncoming freight train loaded with more sorrow.

You did not look around you for answers because you

were sure nobody else understood exactly what you were feeling. No one else could take away your pain. As much as you wanted someone else to come to your rescue, you knew that you had to finally work it out for yourself.

A major piece of your whole frame of life was lost. You could not imagine ever being happy again. You felt as if you had fallen off the merry-go-round of joy and couldn't get back on again. You could not see how life could go on. You desperately needed a way to find hope.

If you have experienced the things I've just described, you understand the true meaning of *personal grief*.

Six months after his wife died of cancer, George said to me, "I'll never be the same again!" The fact is, he was absolutely correct. They had been married 50 years. On the day they celebrated their golden anniversary, she was a well person. A month later cancer was diagnosed and eight months after that she was dead. George had not planned their marriage to end like this. He knew almost 80 percent of the men his age died before their wives. It seemed wrong that she was dead and he was still living. He felt guilty for outliving her.

No one could tell George that life would ever be the same again. He was searching for a glimmer of hope. He came to me to ask if some kind of a life that was worth living was still possible for him. I told George the answer to that question could be found only within his own mind and heart. All I could do was help him learn how to search within himself and encourage him as he made his own discoveries.

Over the next four years George recovered to assume a good life. He started a new hobby of polishing rocks, joined a ballroom dance group and worked as a volunteer with a cancer-support group. His energy level returned to what it was before his wife's death. He ate well and slept well. George was a happy man again.

Susie called me because a friend suggested it. Her boyfriend, Bill, with whom she had been living for three years, had been killed in a motorcycle accident. Susie had left home as a young teenager, married before she was 20, had a child and was divorced. She had moved in with Bill shortly after the divorce was final.

With Bill's death, all of her dreams for herself and her child had been shattered for the second time. She was filled with guilt about the things she ought to have done. She wondered if God was punishing her for her divorce and for living with Bill.

For Susie, as it is for George, life will never be the same again. Susie is also searching for a sign of hope. The direction of her search is inward, for the answers she seeks cannot be found anywhere else.

It is important for Susie to discover that a full life is still possible for her. She must accept the fact that her life is different because of her losses. But she also needs to understand that because her life is different doesn't mean it is ruined. There is life after loss for Susie—and for you.

To deal with a major loss and go on with life you must believe:

❖ *You will live.*

❖ *It's okay for you to live.*

❖ *You can be happy again.*

To believe these things when you have lost a significant piece of your life is a real challenge. But it is possible. And that belief can help you get back on top of life again.

Reflecting on Your Personal Losses

Put these questions on separate pieces of paper. Write your answers to them using as many pages as necessary to fully express your feelings.

❖ *Will I survive the losses I have experienced?*

❖ *Is it okay to go on with my life without whomever or whatever has been lost to me?*

❖ *Can I be happy again knowing that my life will be different because of my losses?*

Read your responses aloud to yourself. See what they are saying about your inner thoughts and feelings.

The more resources you have, including religious beliefs, family traditions and supportive groups, the more fruitful your inward searching will be. The more you understand about what to expect of yourself, the more you will be able to recognize the signs of grief recovery and growth.

On another piece of paper, write down the name of your most recent loss — a person's name or "my marriage," "my home," or whatever best describes the loss. Under the name of your major loss, list the things you've lost as a result of it. For instance, if your spouse died your list might look like this:

Major loss:
    my husband Joe died

Resulting losses:
    financial security
    companionship
    may lose home
    retirement dreams
    close ties with Joe's family
    independence
    sense of personal value

The same kinds of things are often lost if you are dealing with divorce instead of death.

Make your list as complete as possible. Take a look at your resulting losses. Do any of them result in even *more* disappointments? If so, add these to your list.

Notice that whatever loss you experienced caused you to have a *series* of losses. Each one hurts. Each one hits at the core of how you measure your happiness and the value of your life.

Bill was 32 when his wife committed suicide. He said to me, "I didn't just lose a wife. My whole sense of self-worth and all my plans for the future went into the ground with her! What do I do now?"

Nancy, whose husband divorced her after 28 years of marriage, said, "When he walked out the door my security went with him. I've got to find some way to earn a living."

Jack lost everything in a business venture. He said, "I had to learn to see my personal value as separate from my dreams of success before I could give up the idea of killing myself."

Minor Losses

Not all of your losses will be as serious as the death of a loved one, a divorce or a major move. Nevertheless, even so-called minor losses can have a far-reaching impact on your life.

After driving safely for hundreds of thousands of miles, my wife, June and I had two automobile accidents in less than 48 hours. There was no way to avoid either of them. The second was a head-on collision with a truck that crossed the center of the road on a blind curve. June's head hit the windshield. After the impact I looked at her and saw blood squirting from her face, spraying her white pants a bright red.

Within a matter of minutes, people who were total strangers had put her in their car to travel to the nearest hospital several miles away. I remained with our car, waiting for the sheriff to arrive. I had no idea how seriously June was injured or how long it would be before we were together again. By the time I realized I didn't even know the names of the men who had taken her away, June was gone from the scene of the accident.

Over the course of our married life, one of June's pet sayings to me has been, "You take good care of me." I have always enjoyed that vote of confidence. As I stood by our wrecked car and sobbed tears of shock and remorse, I kept muttering, "I didn't take care of her. I didn't take care of her. I lied."

I questioned my decision to stop at a market shortly before the accident. I wondered if there was some way I could have driven the car differently to avoid the collision? What if June was badly hurt? What would I do if she died?

As I think back to that experience, I can identify several losses:

❖ *My identity as June's protector*

❖ *My pride as a skilled driver*

❖ *My sense of security*

❖ *My belief that tragedy happens only to other people*

❖ *My feelings of being in control of life*

I felt an intense sense of grief at simply having to admit our life circumstances were not always in my control.

Fortunately, June was not seriously injured. Expert surgery left only the faintest mark on her freckled nose. However, even though we were very lucky people, it took a year before we had recovered from the effects of that single event in our lives.

Our loss experience was not a major one. No one died. Insurance paid for car repairs. We continue to travel by car as much as ever. The losses we had were minor by comparison to the really terrible things that can happen. Nevertheless, it was important for us to pay attention to the effect this experience has had on our lives.

The failure to recognize these *minor losses* and their impact is one reason people are often so poorly prepared when a major loss occurs. Reflecting on the way smaller losses affect your life can help you prepare for the inevitable major losses that everyone experiences.

If nothing else, paying attention to your smaller losses helps you understand loss is a part of being alive. As you look within yourself to reflect on your response to a smaller loss, you will discover resources that will serve you in times of major loss.

6

Four Key Facts about Grief

Building a foundation for recovery

LEARNING FOUR KEY FACTS about grief will help you take control of it. Accepting these facts will help you develop the stamina and patience you need to endure the burden, stress and time of your grief. They are:

❖ *The way out of grief is through it.*

❖ *The very worst kind of grief is yours.*

❖ *Grief is hard work.*

❖ *Effective grief work is not done alone.*

As you learn to work with grief in these ways, it may feel strange and uncomfortable to you. Perhaps these ideas represent a whole new way for you to think about grief. But, in time and with practice, you will find these concepts to be invaluable tools.

The Way Out of Grief Is Through It

It's a fact! This is the single most important thing for you to learn about grief. If you want to recover from your grief and grow through your loss, you must learn this one fact. There are no shortcuts to a good and full life after a major loss.

Because grief recovery is so demanding, you will look for any way to get out of going through it. None of us wants to face grief. None of us wants to feel the loneliness and heartache it brings. The common tendencies we all have when we experience grief are to:

❖ *Try to avoid it*

❖ *Try to get over it quickly*
   And, when neither of these work,...

❖ *Try to wait it out*

Time heals. How many times have you heard that? But it's not the truth! To say time by itself heals is like saying practice makes perfect. Practice does not make perfect. It is quite possible to practice a perfect mistake. Only *perfect* practice makes perfect! In the same way, only effectively working *through* grief heals the deep wounds and enables you to recover a sense of balance.

Maggie said to me about two years after the death of her husband, "I'll never get over it." We were in a grief support group meeting. As I turned to her I heard myself saying, "Maggie, you're absolutely right! You could work and strain for the next 50 years and you won't get *over* Roy's death. Neither can you get under it or around it. But Maggie, you can always get *through* it!"

If you are tempted to say with Maggie, "I'll never get over it," good for you. You have learned an important truth about grief recovery. An old spiritual, although not written about grief specifically, certainly reflects this important truth. It says:

It's so high you can't get over it,
so low you can't get under it,
so wide you can't get around it,
you must go in through the door.

Whatever other truth these words express, they tell it exactly like it is about the pathway through grief to a full life after any loss.

When you lose a loved one, go through the pain of a divorce or experience some other dramatic change in your life, you do not get over it. That person, place or time of your life will always be a part of you and your personal history.

The more significant your loss is, the greater will be your sense of grief. You will not get over that loss — or under it — nor is there any way around it. You cannot wait it out. You have to go squarely through the middle of it. Learning this is a key to your grief recovery.

Irma, whose husband died 10 years ago, stopped working at her grief about six months after his death. She tried to avoid the sadness by not talking about it. To this day, Irma has never faced her anger at him for dying. As a result, her physical and mental health have suffered. She is plagued by poor health and numerous phobias. It appears now that Irma will not have any lasting sense of joy for the rest of her life.

If you have been through divorce, you know one of the great illusions is that divorce will put an end to problems between spouses. The fact is usually all that changes is you no longer live in the same house.

If you and your ex-spouse fought and argued during

your marriage, you are likely to go on fighting and arguing after your divorce. If you have children, you will continue relating to each other for the rest of your lives. When your children are grown, there are their weddings to attend, grandchildren to love and all the big events in their lives that they want both of you to attend.

Life is too short to spend those years continuing the battles that ended your marriage. The way to achieve peace is to go squarely into the grief that follows the end of a marriage.

You can only do that by facing feelings that are very difficult to face. It has always seemed to me the first casualty in any divorce is the self-esteem of both spouses. This loss alone can knock you flat on your emotional back. It isn't unusual to need as long as a year or more to even begin recovering a healthy self-image.

When one couple divorced after 16 years, the husband was willing to go to a counselor. He worked his way through some very painful discoveries about himself. He learned how he had related to his wife and family in ways that contributed to the breakup of their marriage. He came out of the experience a man changed for the better. He is more patient and understanding. He does not take himself so seriously. He walks through life with a lighter step than before. He is married again and very happy.

For all the sadness, he is able to look back and say that working through his divorce was a good thing. He is grateful it motivated him to grow and change.

His wife, who initiated the divorce, never seemed to face her feelings. She appears to be trying to wait out her sadness. It isn't working. During the three years after their divorce she continued to call on her ex-husband for money, household repairs and emotional support.

Eventually, after he remarried, she moved back into the house they had shared for several years. She seems to be still hanging on to the symbols of a relationship that is over. She has tried to avoid grieving its loss. In the meantime, the need to grieve just waits—and grows!

To go through grief takes both stamina and an incredible amount of patience. At some time along the way, you will feel terribly sad, lonely, lost, angry—or all of these. If you are to get in touch with such unpleasant feelings, you must have a strong sense of purpose and direction. You have to be totally convinced there is absolutely no other way out of your grief than straight through the middle of it.

It isn't unusual or abnormal to feel more uncomfortable after confronting your grief. It should be expected. But that isn't worse—it's better!

Many times after one of our grief support group meetings one of the participants will call to say, "I felt worse when I left than when I came in." The caller is often shocked when I respond, "Good for you! It means you're growing."

Feeling better comes a day, a week or a few months later. If you are working through a major loss and feel comfortable, it's a danger signal. It's time to check to see if you are trying to skirt the flank, dig under or get over your grief. It's a fact: You can't!

Going through the experience is the only way out of grief that is lasting and healthy.

Throughout this book you will find exercises that provide effective ways to handle the feelings that emerge as you move through your grief and establish a new life after your loss.

The Very Worst Kind of Grief Is Yours

Which grief experience is the worst? Is it more difficult for the widow if her husband suddenly and unexpectedly drops dead of a heart attack? Or is it worse if he dies an inch at a time from cancer? Is it worse to lose a spouse to death or a marriage through divorce? Is the death of a child the worst of all losses? All of these are irrelevant questions. There is only one very worst kind of grief and that is *yours!*

In one winter two disastrous events happened at the same time, each of which made an impact on my life. First, a number of men were killed in a mining accident. My sister called because she knew some of the families. That tragedy made headline news everywhere. The other tragic event was having our 15-year-old cat "put to sleep."

Can you guess which of those events caused me to cry my eyes out? You guessed it—the cat!

There is scarcely any comparison between the loss of human life and the end of a semi-crippled old cat. But Samantha was *my* cat. I loved her. She was a permanent part of our history. Her loss was not an academic thing. I didn't look at television or newspaper accounts of her death and say, "That's too bad!" and go on to the sports page. She was mine. Her loss plunged me into grief.

I stood in the front room of our home as my wife drove off with the cat to the veterinarian to have the dastardly deed done. I couldn't walk into that office and fall apart in tears. Everyone knows big boys, especially professional clergymen, don't do that sort of thing. So—I let my wife do it! I held Samantha briefly, tickling her under the chin in the way she liked so much, then carried her out to the car where June was waiting.

As she drove off I screamed and sobbed, crying out over and over again, "I want my kitty. I don't want her to die!"

This was my loss and at that moment, as far as I was concerned, it was the worst thing to happen in the whole world. I didn't want anyone to tell me how great it was that she didn't suffer, or how far beyond a normal life expectancy she had lived.

I wasn't very objective about the loss of Samantha as compared to the mining disaster, or the loss of my parents some years earlier or the starving masses in the Third

World. Grief is like that. It isn't helped by saying, "How childishly you are behaving over a cat!"

I have known deeper times of grief—much deeper. A neighbor girl, who grew up spending as much time in our home as her own, committed suicide at 19. My mother and father are both dead. I have held the hands of friends as they died, baptized stillborn infants, helped families decide when to disconnect life-support systems and worked with parents whose children were murdered.

Each of those experiences was painful. Nevertheless, at the moment my cat died, her loss was the very worst kind of grief for me in the whole world.

Think about your own experience. Perhaps you sold one home and bought a new one. You were very excited as moving day approached, only to find yourself standing in the empty old house after the last box was gone, overwhelmed with a deep sense of loss and sadness. As one man said, "it is as if you have divorced your house." That feeling of sadness is grief. And at that moment, for you, it was the very worst kind of grief simply because it was yours.

The death of even the most aged family member hurts because the loss is yours. Rabbi Earl Grollman's father was past 90. His health had been poor for years. He was an invalid confined to a rest home. When he died, a well-meaning friend said to Earl, "He had a long and good life. Aren't you glad his suffering is over now?" Earl says he replied in a voice that did not mask his anger, "You don't understand. *My daddy just died!*"

Never apologize for grieving. Remind yourself as often as needed that the very worst kind of loss is always yours.

Learn to acknowledge that your loss is worthy of grief. Whatever your experience is, you must endure your very real feelings of sadness and anger on the way to recovering a full life once more. If you are going to come out of grief a better person, you cannot be concerned about how you ought to feel on the way through it.

When Phyliss came to our grief support group, she had lost her daughter, son-in-law and three grandchildren in a bizarre mass murder. Two years later, her husband died of cancer. By contrast, Susan came only because her widower father needed her to bring him. A year later, he died. Susan continued to come alone after the funeral. One day she said, "I feel guilty for feeling so sad. My loss seems so insignificant compared to Phyliss' loss."

That attitude could have been a stumbling block to Susan's grief recovery. It was important for her to know that her grief was just as real as that of Phyliss.

It hurts to lose important persons, places and things from your life experience. The correct and appropriate response is grief. If you don't acknowledge your loss and begin to work your way through it, even small grief experiences begin to stack up. They become like bills waiting to be paid—and piling up interest.

As long as you tell yourself you shouldn't feel as you do, or pretend you don't hurt, the loss stays with you. Recovery begins when you admit that no matter what other tragedies exist in the world, at this very moment, the very worst kind of grief is yours.

You do not owe an apology to friends, family or God for grieving the loss of anything or anybody. If others understand, that's nice. If they don't, it's too bad.

The way out of grief is through it. And, the way through it begins by acknowledging that your loss is worthy of grief, even if it's an old cat.

Grief Is Hard Work

Making your way through grief is called *doing grief work.* I never fully appreciated what that means until I immersed myself in other people's grief experiences. There is no better way to describe the things you will endure than the word *work*. Grieving is work. It is the most difficult work any of us will ever do.

Viewing grief as work will help you not try to wait it out. It will help you keep from looking to others to be responsible for making you feel whole again.

Some tasks just can't be given to someone else. Nobody can do the work of acknowledging the death of your loved one for you. Nobody else can do the very difficult task of saying good-bye and releasing that person, that relationship, that part of your body, or whatever it is you have lost. You must do that for yourself.

The following image helps me understand the work dimension of grief.

Suppose you have had a group of friends over for a spaghetti dinner. It's been a delightful evening, but now your guests have gone home. You walk into your kitchen, and there sit the dishes. Those tomato-sauce-turned-to-glue-covered dishes are one of the truly ugly sights in the world!

You're tired and in the mood for anything but washing dishes. You now have two basic choices: You can leave the mess until morning. Or, you can wash the dishes now regardless of how you feel.

If you leave them, the present moment is certainly more pleasant. In fact, the balance of the evening can be delightful and your night's rest refreshing. But come daylight, there they are! Now those dishes are uglier than ever as they stare at you with mute disdain.

Now, the task is even more difficult. The pleasantness of the dinner party is gone and forgotten as you face the same decision again: Do you wash them now, put off the gruesome task until some other time, or hope the tooth fairy will come along and wash them for you?

If you choose to wash the dishes immediately after dinner, your guests just might help you—if you're lucky.

At worst, you have a tough evening and go to bed exhausted. But come morning, the task is finished. You can go on to the new day basking in the warmth of a good evening and the knowledge that you did good work with a difficult task.

Grief work is much like that image. There is work that must be done at a time when you feel like doing nothing at all. Grief work can be put off. You can feel better for awhile by avoiding some feelings and not talking about some things. But there will be a day when you awaken to see that your feelings are still there and things still need to be talked about with someone who understands and cares.

Like those dinner dishes, the longer you wait, the more difficult and unpleasant grief work becomes. Grief is not an illness. But if you try to avoid grief work, you may well become sick.

Dr. Glen Davidson's research showed about 25 percent of those who mourn experience a dramatic decrease in their bodies' immune system six to nine months after their loss. That lack of immunity accounts in part for the higher rate of illness when we are grieving.

The research also demonstrated that this immune system deficiency is totally avoidable. If you do the work of grieving, including taking care of your physical and emotional needs, you will be okay.

The first thing you need is a support group with whom you can talk freely. Then you must pay attention to the foods you eat, the amount and kinds of fluids you drink, getting adequate exercise and sufficient rest.

It's hard work. There is much to do and only you can do much of it.

Effective Grief Work Is Not Done Alone

One of the worst myths you will hear about grief goes like this:

❖ *Grief is such a personal thing it should be kept to yourself.*

Another is:

❖ *Nobody else can help. You have to handle your own grief.*

Nothing could be further from the truth!

It is another fact of life and loss that effective grief work is not done alone.

Your grief should never be a private affair. You need other people as much as you need air to breathe. You need to talk about your experiences and your feelings. You need to listen to others share about what's happening to them. There is more than comfort in such sharing. There is the strength you need to endure the length and burden of your grief.

If you keep your grief to yourself, you run an unnecessary risk of having it becoming distorted. Joe dropped out of our grief support group after coming twice. He said he wasn't willing to come week after week and cry in front of a bunch of women. The last I knew he was still struggling with blackouts and ulcers. He married again less than a year after his wife's death. His new wife has been to see me several times to talk about his moodiness. Joe refuses to come with her.

Jane could never tell the group that her marriage had not been the idyllic romance she had wanted it to be. Neighbors and friends knew about the loud arguments and alcohol problems. But after her husband's death she talked about their relationship as if it had been made in heaven. After a few months, she became increasingly hostile and unwilling to share her feelings. Her participation in the group was limited to giving advice to others. In time, she dropped out altogether. For awhile, she attended other grief groups in the city, none of which satisfied her. Four years after her husband's death Jane was still a very bitter, unhappy person.

The saddest fact about Joe and Jane is their problems could have been avoided. You can move through your grief experience and come out a healthy person. To do that, however, there must be other people involved in your life and your grief.

The Power of Shared Experiences

Of all the groups in our church, my favorite is the grief support group. I can't imagine a more sensitive and caring group of people anywhere. Nowhere else have I seen the age barrier disappear more quickly. There is something very special about seeing a young mother whose baby was stillborn and an 80-year-old widow taking care of each other.

Those who share such deep places together become a real help to others. They seem to instinctively know the right words to say to a newly bereaved person. They know the time to speak and the time when words are neither adequate or necessary.

The more social your grief work is, the better you will do with it. The more you talk about it publicly, write about it in letters and share in the grief of others, the more effectively you will adapt to your own loss. Nobody is saying it's easy. It is only necessary.

Men and Grief

Men seem to have more difficulty sharing grief experiences than women. Some of this reluctance probably has to do with our masculine dread of emotionalism. Many of us have grown up with the silly notion that tears are a sign of weakness and lack of character. The price for such foolishness has proven to be very high.

A man I know has been on the brink of bankruptcy for several years. In the past he was a successful businessman.

He and his family lived in more than moderate comfort in a fine home. His attempt to expand into a new venture led to the loss of their business and their home. They are faced with starting all over again.

Outwardly, he seems to be holding up very well. But he doesn't want to talk about his feelings with anyone. He could be growing through his loss. He could be having the strong support of people who would understand his feelings. He could be on his way to recovery. He isn't. By keeping it all to himself, his risk of serious illness is many times higher than normal.

Men have the same basic needs for healthy grief recovery as women. This includes the need to be with others who have had similar losses and to talk openly about what is happening to each one.

If you are male and have had a major loss in your life, don't try to handle it alone. If you are too uncomfortable meeting with a group of women, a little investigation will uncover other men who share your feelings. Get together for breakfast or lunch on a weekly basis. Use this book as a guide for your discussions.

Careless Things People Say

Almost every divorced person and every widow or widower I know has had someone say something that can only be called *cruel*. Bereaved persons are often rejected for crying and rewarded for keeping a bright smile, even when it is killing them. Divorced men and women discover friends taking sides and making judgments at a time when what they need most is a friendly ear.

Numerous widows have shared experiences with me of being forgotten by social or church groups after the death of their spouses. After her husband's death, Maggie gathered up the courage to go back to a bridge club in which they had been members for several years. It was a difficult step for her to take. The bridge club was an activity she and Roy had always shared. When Maggie arrived, she was greeted at the door by a long-time friend who said, "My dear, don't you know this is for couples?"

It doesn't take more than one experience like that to convince you it is better to keep grief to yourself!

You will find people, including some doctors and clergy, who are too uncomfortable with grief to reach out to you. Friends may avoid you because they don't know what to say. Co-workers may be afraid they will say something that upsets you, so they say nothing at all. It often seems as if there is a conspiracy of silence whenever you are present.

Like most grieving persons, you will probably come to hate the question, "How are you?" You will discover very quickly that the only acceptable answer is "fine," regardless of how miserable you are feeling at the moment.

Nevertheless, it remains a fact that effective grief work is not done alone. For this reason it is vitally important for you to find a counselor or a support group who will listen. In almost every community there are such resources simply because loss is such a universal human experience. In Appendix C you will find guidelines for forming a grief support group if one is not available.

[1] Glen W. Davidson. *Understanding Mourning*, pp.24-27.

7

The Time to Start Is Now

No one else can do it for you

I KEEP THIS QUOTATION by an unknown author pinned to a bulletin board over my desk:

There will never be another now —
  I'll make the most of today.
There will never be another me —
  I'll make the most of myself.

It's a good motto for doing effective grief work. The only time you have to start working through your losses is today. Tomorrow will not be a better day to face up to the task. The only one who can make the journey through your grief is you. But as you make it, you will discover you are equal to the challenge.

Doing grief work, in one sense, is a little bit like making love—talking about it can take you only so far—it is finally something you must do. Admittedly, there is nothing pleasurable about grief. But if you learn the skills of effective grief work, you can emerge from your losses with a great sense of satisfaction.

The time to start working on grief is now. If you have experienced a major loss, it won't help to wait for some other day when you feel better to get started working on it. The potential risk to your health and the absence of joy from your life are prices too high to pay for postponing the task.

Exercises that Help

This book contains exercises that can help you handle any loss in your life. Each exercise has something for you to do that focuses on a specific step to grief recovery. Not all of the exercises will apply to you at this moment. However, all of them are worth your attention.

For instance, exercises on handling grief after divorce are also applicable to other losses. With minor adjustments, those that focus on death will apply to divorce or relocation. If the particular loss addressed doesn't fit your experience, there is a good chance it applies to someone you know who needs your understanding and help.

It is important to remember that you will not move through grief in an orderly, well-defined manner. A task that seems completed three months after loss may have to be done again many times. If this is your experience, it is not a setback, but a perfectly normal way for grief to progress.

The important thing is that you are facing your loss and working through your grief. It will be tempting to try an end run around the pain of grief or to withdraw and wait it out. Neither of these approaches will work.

Doing the exercises will help you continue moving through your grief, which is the only way through it.

Applying the Four Key Facts to Your Grief

As a warm-up to doing other exercises, copy each of the Four Key Facts about Grief onto a separate piece of paper. List each fact at the top of the page and then list ways it applies to your grief experience. For instance, you might head one sheet, *the way out of grief is through it.* Under this, list things you can do to go through your experience and things to avoid that represent an effort to side-step your grief. You could remind yourself to talk to someone about your loss every day and write a description of the feelings you are having.

You need to work with the four key facts until you are clear about the way each of them applies to your loss and grief. As you become more comfortable with the truths they offer, you will be able to see more of the potential for a full and rewarding life after your loss.

❖ *The way out of grief is through it.*

❖ *The very worst kind of grief is yours.*

❖ *Grief is hard work.*

❖ *Effective grief work is not done alone.*

Understanding and accepting these key facts about grief recovery is crucial to building a rewarding life after a major loss.

A Recent Life History Survey

This exercise is for everybody. It will help you identify loss experiences that may have seemed insignificant at the time they happened, but which could be continuing to affect your happiness today.

Take a survey

Answer the questions in the sequence in which they are presented. Answer all the questions before going on to the instructions that follow the survey.

1. List the most significant changes in your life during the past two years. Include such positive experiences as job promotions, new home, getting married (or having children married), retirement or graduating from college. Negative experiences will include a death in the family, divorce, loss of job, surgery, serious illness, moving from familiar surroundings or business failure.

2. Diagram your moods over the past year: happy (contented); okay (some ups and downs); or sad (depressed, discontented).

	Jan	Feb	Mar	Apr	May	Jun	Jul	Aug	Sep	Oct	Nov	Dec
Happy												
Okay												

3. List any physical problems have you had in the last 18 months.

4. Describe your outlook on life right now in terms of:
   A color
   A taste
   A smell
   A touch
   A sound

5. Write down the one thing in your life you would change at this moment if you could. (Describe the way you think it is and the way you would like it to be.)

Examine your responses

After you have completed the survey, read back through your answers. As you examine your responses:

1. Ask yourself, "What losses did I experience in each of the major changes I listed?"

2. "Which of these losses continues to make the greatest impact on my life?" As you think about this loss, what feelings do you have? Refer to the list of feeling words in Appendix A for help in naming your feelings.

3. Check the diagram of your moods over the last year. Is there any correlation between your moods at various times and the loss you have identified?

Focus on the saddest of your moods and try to remember what was happening at each of those times.

Identify your losses in each of those experiences and name your feelings about them.

4. What was happening during the times of your happiest moods? What feelings can you name about those experiences? In what way were you in control of your own destiny at those times?

5. Look at your list of physical problems. Is there any correlation between these problems and the loss experiences you have named?

List the approximate time your physical symptoms were noticed. Measure back six months, nine months, one year and 18 months from this time. Note the events in your life around each of these times. Was there a loss involved? If so, what was it and is that loss still affecting your life today?

6. Do your physical problems keep you from doing anything you would otherwise do if you didn't have a limitation?

If so, describe what you would do if you could. What sense of loss do you feel because you cannot do that thing?

7. Look at the words you used to describe your present outlook on life. Do you like these images?

Is the color your favorite?

Is the taste something you like?

Is the smell pleasant?

Is the touch pleasurable?

Is the sound one you would like to hear again?

How do you feel about your answers in each category? Do they indicate a positive or negative outlook on life?

If your outlook is more negative than positive, ask yourself, "What have I lost recently that, if it were given back to me, would make my outlook on life more positive?"

8. Think about the thing you would most like to change in your life. Is it possible to realize that change?

You can't get back a loved one who has died, a divorced spouse who has remarried, a limb or organ lost to surgery or a special time in your life. Recovering just about every other loss is possible, regardless of how improbable that recovery might be.

9. If the one change you would make is not possible, you have grief work to do. Identify the focus of your grief. Don't try to fool yourself or name a loss that feels respectable to you. For instance, if you are divorcing and it is not the loss of your spouse that hurts, but the loss of your children or self-esteem, say so. Focus your grief on *that* loss.

10. If the change you would make is possible, ask yourself, "Why haven't I already made that change? What is holding me back?"

Does the change require the participation of someone else? Who? Have you talked with that person about it?

Knowing that for every change, there is a price to be paid, what is the price for the change you would like to make? Are you willing to pay that price?

Talking It Over

To get the most benefit from the survey, first go through it carefully by yourself and then share your findings with a trusted friend, family member, counselor or clergy. The simple act of talking about your loss and feelings is an important step to recovery.

Your loss may seem so small that you are embarrassed to make an issue of it. If so, remember the second key fact about grief recovery: The very worst kind of loss is *yours.*

It is important to pay particular attention to any correlation between your physical problems and a time of loss. You can spend a great deal of time and money treating physical symptoms and never get to the root cause if loss and grief are factors of your illness. If you suspect there might be a connection, you need a psychologist or clergyperson and a doctor who understand the relationship of grief and illness.

Guidelines for Doing Grief Work

Once you have identified your losses, the next step is to begin the work of recovering your balance. The following guidelines will help get you started and keep you going when you grow weary of the task.

Believe that your grief has a purpose and an end

Trust that you will make it through. It is a fact that grief is work to be done. It is also a fact that there is an end to the work. In the early going I can only ask you to take my word for it. You will probably think your sadness is going on forever. It won't. Later, that will become evident to you as you do the things I suggest.

Earlier I compared grief work with washing dishes. Once you have washed dishes, that work is finished until you use the dishes again. Grief work is like that. Once you have done the work required for you to regain your balance, it is finished until you experience another loss. The more you learn about grief the better you can handle it.

Nobody wants to be good at grieving. We are half afraid if the word gets out that we know how, something awful will happen. We would much prefer to do without the experience of grief altogether. But life doesn't work that way. Because you will not be spared from times of loss, it is important to believe that your grief has a purpose.

If your outlook on life is upbeat and healthy, you have a basic trust that life is good. When you experience a major loss, that sense of basic trust is shaken. You will question whether life is not actually chaotic and unfair. In truth, sometimes it is!

Shortly after our marriage, my wife and I were awakened in the middle of the night in our third-floor apartment by a strong earthquake. We awoke feeling nauseated, disoriented and scared to death. The room was swaying back and forth!

The sensible thing to have done would have been to immediately get up and crouch in a doorway. Instead, we were paralyzed by fear and distrust of our environment. We laid in bed holding tight to each other until the movement subsided.

When a major loss occurs in your life, that same kind of shaking of your reality and security takes place. Being paralyzed by fear and distrust isn't going to get you back on balance. But it's hard to get moving. You need to believe there is a purpose to all that is happening.

I don't mean there is some purpose for your loss. If you believe your loss has happened to teach you some lesson or to punish you, the work of recovery will be more difficult. It is better to accept the fact that some things happen to us and our loved ones for no reason at all. Some things, including tragedies, just happen. This world is dependable and one of the things you can depend on is loss and grief.

One of the most common questions I hear from bereaved persons is "What have I done wrong? Is this a punishment?" It's certainly an understandable question. But it is also a foolish one for which there is no good answer except "no." Bad things happen to bad people *and* to good people. Loss and grief are not inflicted upon you or anyone else by design. They happen because you are alive in a mortal and imperfect world.

To grow through loss you have to learn that the fact of loss does not diminish life.

Be responsible for your own grief process

A motto for success used by many super-achievers goes like this:

If it is to be, it is up to me.

That's a great motto for grief recovery!

No one can do your grieving for you. No one else can make your decisions or feel your feelings or cry tears that are essential for recovering from major loss. That's one reason why it is so important for you to see grief not as an illness from which to recover, but as old-fashioned hard work that you must do.

You will find the most difficult time to stay responsible for your grief recovery is when depression hits. When your sadness is dominated by fatigue and when things that normally bring joy don't stir you, it is very hard to feel responsible for anything.

Depression can become so intense that you require medication. If it persists long enough, you may need to be hospitalized. But even then, it is finally you who must choose to come out of the depression.

Depression is a way of taking time out from working through grief. It's like lifting a barbell over your head. Perhaps you can lift it once, twice, or 10 times. But there comes a time when the weight is too heavy and your muscles are too fatigued to lift it once more. At that moment you have no choice but to rest your arms before trying to lift it again.

It is important to know when you need to relax and divert yourself from doing grief work.

It is important that you aren't quitting grief work too soon. If you take time out you need a plan for getting back to work.

Throughout the process of your grief work, you will do the best if you maintain a personal responsibility for completing it.

Don't be afraid to ask for help

To ask for help is not giving up responsibility for your grief. It is recognizing that lifting yourself by the shoestrings usually results in a hernia or broken shoestrings—not lifting you off the floor!

Remember one of the key facts about grief recovery: Effective grief work is not done alone. You need others when trying to work your way out of the sadness and depression that follow a major loss.

The most useful part of our grief support program is not the weekly meetings in my office, but the support people give each other in between sessions. We publish a roster of those who attend. Men and women on the list who are willing to be available in a time of special need are indicated by an asterisk. They are called frequently by others in the program.

It is the security of knowing there is somebody always available who understands grief that makes the program work. Sometimes the simplest of acts counts the most. Two of our older widows were each finding their evening dinner to be the loneliest time of the day. Neither of them was eating properly or regularly.

One woman drives a car on a limited basis, the other

not at all. By mapping out a route that kept them off of the busiest streets, I was able to arrange for the one who drives to pick up the other to dine at a local cafeteria on a regular basis. Within two weeks I saw marked improvements in their energy levels and outlooks.

You should not be afraid to ask for help, but it is important for the person you ask to understand the grief recovery process. The best of all support will come from others who are working through their own losses. You can find such people in every community.

I was a guest speaker at a church one Sunday. The minister announced that I would be available to meet on the following Tuesday with anyone who had experienced a major loss. A full 10 percent of the congregation showed up for the meeting.

Experiences like this have taught me that loss and grief are universal experiences. Given an opportunity to share and the promise of an open, accepting atmosphere, many people will respond.

If you look for others who are as eager as you to work through loss and grief, you will have no trouble finding them. If you can find a leader who is trained in grief and loss, that's a bonus. If you can't, just gather a group and use this book for your guide. Appendix C gives you specific guidelines for forming a group and directing the first 12 sessions.

Don't rush it

I am not known for my patience. One of my dear friends, an 80-year-old widow who "adopted" me after the death of her husband, calls me "Reverend Buzz Bomb." It's a title that causes me to wince only because of its accuracy. I have always believed the best time to accomplish anything was yesterday. I walk fast, talk fast and eat fast, much to my wife's disdain! I live in the high-speed lane and wouldn't have it any other way. The most difficult thing about writing this book was that there was no way to rush it.

I have much sympathy with those of you who have problems being patient with your grief. However, with all the compassion I can muster, I must tell you this: Grief work can't be rushed. It will take at least two or three years to work through a death or divorce.

Irene, about whom I wrote earlier, worked as hard as anyone I know to get through the death of her husband. She said to me soon after his death, "Bob, I don't intend to let my grief own me! I intend to attack it with everything I've got and to seek all the help I can get. It may take others two or three years, but not me!"

She did attack her grief. Irene never tried to avoid any part of it, or any feeling that came with it. She was able to cry openly. She poured herself into helping others in the grief support group. She sought the help of one of the best psychologists in our city. I can't think of one thing Irene could have done that she didn't do.

When she said to me one Sunday, "I have to tell you, it doesn't hurt anymore," two years and nine months had passed. The process just can't be rushed. It will take more time than you think you can bear, but you can and you will.

Some of your friends and some of your family will disappoint you along the way. Actually, "disappoint" is a polite word for "destroy." Grief is almost as frightening to the non-grieving person as it is to the one who is grieving. To move through grief and recover your balance takes patience—lots of it—first with yourself, and then with others.

More Things to Do

After you complete the survey at the beginning of this chapter share it with at least two other people.

Write each of the four statements listed below on a 3x5 card. Concentrate on one of them each day. On the back of the card, outline what you think that statement means for your grief experience. Share those insights with four different people.

Here are the statements:

❖ *I believe my grief has a purpose and an end.*

❖ *I will be responsible for my own grief process.*

❖ *I will not be afraid to ask for help.*

❖ *I will not try to rush my recovery.*

8

Growing
Through Loss

Meeting life's great test

W̲E ALL KNOW THAT GRIEF is about losing. We
need to know that it can also be about growing.

During the first weeks and months after a death, divorce or any major loss in your life, you need to be
reminded many times that you will not always feel as you
do at the moment. You may think the pain of your loss will
never go away. It may seem as if the feelings of sadness
and emptiness will last forever. You may think you have
smiled for the last time in your life. To have these thoughts
and feelings is quite normal. The truth is, the pain will
diminish, the sadness will leave and laughter will return.

If you work at it, the grieving process can become a
time of growth. If you do not try to avoid grieving, but face

it head-on, you can get back on top of life again. The way out of grief may not be a nice, neat stair-climb, but there is a way to conquer it. Your path to recovery will have many ups and downs, but if you stay with it, you will emerge stronger than when you started.

You need to know that some of the downs you can expect will come after several months, even a year or more. There is no magic time when everything will be okay again. If you know what to expect, you can avoid being harsh on yourself and adding to your own sadness. You don't need to fall into the needless trap of thinking, "I am the only one who feels this way."

For instance, you may reach a point, perhaps six months after your loss, when you feel better. You will begin to function more normally—sleep better, food will taste better and you will perform routine tasks as you did before your loss. Days will go along fairly smoothly. Then, something will "come off the wall" to hit you. You may hear a familiar song on the radio or see a person walking on the street who bears a striking resemblance to your deceased spouse. Perhaps you hear that your divorced mate is about to remarry or that someone has been named to fill your old job. Whatever it is that happens, your response is to have the roof cave in on your emotions.

When this happens, it is common to think you have slipped and are starting your grieving all over again. That simply isn't true. You are exactly where you should be.

Many people have the same experience. A widow said, "Hitting a low just shows how far up you have already been." You need to see these upsets as mileposts along the way to grief recovery and signs of personal growth. They aren't setbacks, they are signs of forward movement. They will happen again.

I have led grief support groups for years. Some folks have come to a group for the first time 18 months after the death of a spouse because, in their words, "I thought

I was doing so well until one day I felt as if I were starting all over again."

When something like that happens, remind yourself that grief is not a bad word. It isn't something you shouldn't feel. There is no certain emotional place you have to be at a given time.

The inevitable emotional upheavals are surefire signs that you are doing fine. If you continue to face your grief and work your way through your loss, you *will* come out at the other end a stronger person than when you started.

One of the exercises you will find in a later chapter is designed to help you see that grief is manageable. It lets you personalize your sense of loss by writing a letter that begins, "Dear Grief." When you write, describe whatever it is you would like to say to your grief, if you could stand before it face-to-face.

The exercise continues with a second letter, written 24 hours later. This letter will be from your grief to you. It describes whatever it is you think your grief is trying to communicate to you.

I have seen marvelous healing and growth begin with this simple act of letter writing.

Four months after her husband's death, Irene wrote the following:

Dear Grief,

You are a rascal. You take our energy, our organizational abilities and our brains and do strange things with them. I was prepared for the immediate grief and to feel the loss of my spouse for a long, long time. I was not prepared for the laziness, low energy level, and the stress.

I am impatient with it all. You take so much out of us when we really need to be able to function well. I do not understand why.

*I must confess you've done good things for me
also. I am more compassionate, understanding,
tolerant. You have given me new ways to be of
service and God will show me those ways. Perhaps
after I've had more time to look back I will feel
differently about you, but for right now you are
not one of my favorite friends. I am a better person
because of you and I must not lose sight of that.*

Sincerely,
Irene

A day later she wrote this letter to herself from her
grief:

Dear Irene,

*I'm sorry I've caused you so much pain. Remem-
ber that your pastor said at the funeral, "Grief is
the noblest emotion of all." It truly is the last gift
of love you can give your husband. So experience
it in a normal way. Let your own time frame
happen.*

*I know you are working hard to get through this
phase of your life. I commend you for that. But, I
also want to say "Let go and let God." Just put it in
God's hands. I suggest you read the verses on death
in the Bible. Remember, there is an atomic bomb
of hope waiting to explode between the front and
back covers of your Bible. I sense your excitement
as you search through those scriptures. You may
be truly amazed at what you find.*

*Begin to use your time more wisely. Get extra sleep
once or twice a week. You'll be all right. Soon your
energy level will return. You may even lose the
weight you've been trying to lose for some time. In
time you will walk lighter. You will sit lighter. You*

will feel great.

I am your friend. I am a part of life. There is a purpose for me. You will see.

Sincerely,
Grief

The attitude Irene expressed toward her grief in those letters was the key to her return to a full and productive life. She is again a person with a zest for living and an energy level that sparkles. She is positive, outgoing and healthy. Irene has successfully handled a terrible loss. She has also been a great help to dozens of others at times of similar losses.

One Sunday Irene took me by the arm after church and said, "I have to tell you. It doesn't hurt anymore. I can enjoy the memories of our life together without having my enjoyment canceled by the pain of losing him. I am ready to live the rest of my life fully now."

That moment and the shine in Irene's eyes remains one of my all-time greatest memories. It will be a source of hope whenever my own next grief experience comes.

Grief is always about losing. People like Irene have taught me that it can also be about growing and winning. The kind of personal growth Irene experienced is possible for you too as you work through your losses.

I first began to connect grief and growth when I started meeting regularly with a group of bereaved people. As they talked about the many facets of their grief experience, I felt some of the incredible depth of sadness that accompanies such losses.

But there was something else present, too. I saw those people laugh together at how forgetful one can become under the stress of grief. I saw new skills, talents and compassion emerge from one person after another. A strong sense of unity developed between those people as they shared experiences with each other. "I didn't know anyone else did that" became a weekly motto for the group.

A widow went back to school and is now enjoying the career she always wanted, but which she put aside for many years to be home with her husband.

A man who, in his own words, "couldn't successfully boil water," joined a cooking class at a community college after his wife's death. He now prepares gourmet meals for friends.

Several people learned they could do mechanical things they never thought possible before their spouse's death. There was a sense throughout the group that life had put each one to the ultimate test, and each was able to meet it!

This is what it means to grow through loss:

❖ *Growth means gaining a new love and reverence for life.*

❖ *It means shifting your attention from the ordinary to the quality elements of life.*

❖ *Growth is a greater awareness of our mutual need for each other and a greater sense of the sacred dimension of life.*

I have never seen this kind of growth happen as a result of winning a lottery, achieving success in business or reaping a windfall of any kind. I see it weekly in persons who are working their way through loss and grief.

That doesn't mean grief is an experience to be treasured. None of us wants to feel the horrible emptiness and desolation that comes with a major loss. Yet we need to understand that feelings of grief won't hurt us if we face them and work our way through them. Working through loss can also mean growing through loss. The depths of grief hurt, but it can be a creative hurt.

When our first grandchild was born, our daughter-in-law and son chose to have it by natural childbirth. They went through training classes and when the time of birth came, he was with her in the delivery room as her "coach." We waited outside the door with the other eager grand-parents-to-be. Within a few minutes of our grand-daugh-ter's arrival, we were ushered in to see mother and baby.

Our daughter-in-law's first words were, "I'll never do it again this way, it hurt too much!" An hour later the mem-ory of the pain was just a part of the total experience of creating a new life. By the next day it was something she had met and conquered. They have since had two more children by the same method. That's *creative hurt*.

The pain of grief can also be creative hurt. It is real and long-lasting, but it is not permanent. It passes. Not only does it pass, but it can help create new life along the way.

The most helpful person to a newly widowed person is another widow or widower. When Irene goes to call on a new widow in our church, she has something to offer that I cannot give. Her presence as one who has survived the experience and come out on top says there is real hope for others. I might *say* there is hope. Irene has *lived* it.

Over and over again, I have seen one widow anticipate the exact day and hour that another widow needs to receive a telephone call and a word of encouragement. It is no coincidence. Once you have been there you know what is happening, when it happens, and what needs to be done.

Likewise, no one else can listen to someone in the midst of a divorce like the person who has been there and made it through.

"I know how you feel" can be words of comfort or can sound like fingernails across a chalkboard. It depends on whether the one speaking them has the experience to back them up. It also requires a sensitive understanding that no one ever really knows exactly how another person is feeling—especially about something as emotionally loaded as a major loss.

Some years ago, when the aerospace industry went through one of its many cutbacks, several men in our church lost their jobs. They were engineers and lab technicians who were well educated and who performed their jobs with skill. Being unemployed was the last thing on their minds until it happened.

A very astute businessman saved the day for many of them. He gathered these men into a sharing and support group. There they were free to talk about how terrible it felt to be laid off and how much their sense of self-worth was hurting. They didn't have to be strong with each other as they thought they had to do at home and in church. They gave each other acceptance and encouragement as one after another retrained for a new work field. About two years after it started, the group disbanded because it was no longer needed.

Those men experienced grief as a result of losing their jobs, dreams and a sense of self-esteem. No one could help them through it better than they could help each other.

You can decide to grow through the most devastating loss in your life! A major part of the growing side of grief is coming to understand that, in the midst of a life-changing loss, we still have control over our own destiny. You may not be able to choose all of the circumstances of your life, but you can always choose your responses to anything that happens.

I urge you to begin now.

What loss have you had recently? Think back over the past two years.

❖ *When have you had periods of sadness?*

❖ *What was happening at those times?*

❖ *Make a list of your losses. Read it aloud.*

❖ *What feelings do you have as you hear yourself announcing your losses?*

❖ *Make a list of your strongest feelings. Read through the list of "feeling words" in Appendix A to express yourself more clearly.*

❖ *Have you had occasions when it seemed that other people were more critical or uncaring toward you?*

❖ *Have you had any illnesses?*

❖ *Are any of your family relationships more stressed than usual?*

All of these things can be signs of unresolved grief in your life. All of them are occasions of loss. *You* can also make them into occasions of growth.

To achieve the happiness you would like for yourself, pay attention to your losses and begin working through your grief. The process takes time to learn and will take a lifetime to do.

Fortunately, a lifetime is exactly what we have been given for the task.

9

A Contest
of Endurance

Life after loss takes time

OF ALL THE CHALLENGES YOU FACE in working through grief none is more demanding than the endurance it requires.

If your spouse or child has died, you can't bear to think recovering from that loss is going to take as long as three years. But rarely is it less and often it is much longer.

No newly divorced person wants to think in terms of two or more years before recovering from a lost love. It takes at least that long if you work hard. Many try to fill the void by immediately getting involved with another person. It doesn't work and it can be dangerous to your future health. Having a new love is not a substitute for working through the grief of losing a former love.

The length of your grief after any major loss will be considerably longer than you expect. It takes a long time to work through the various steps of recovery. To endure the time it takes you must believe the rewards are worth the effort. You must also know that trying to rush the process is an exercise in futility—and can lengthen the time required for you to recover your sense of balance.

The Weight of Grief is Heavy

Fatigue is one of the most common symptoms of people working through grief. Grief is heavy. Carrying its weight is tiring. People tell me they are constantly exhausted in the first three to six months after a death or divorce.

When Dick lost a business because of an unscrupulous partner, he spent a solid week in bed, too weary to bathe or get dressed.

After a major loss, if you are so tired that everything you do is an effort, you are reacting in a normal way. It's a heavy load and it takes an incredible amount of endurance to carry it.

The stress of carrying the load of your grief may result in feelings of depression. You may have little interest in eating regularly or paying attention to the nutritional balance of your meals. If you are like most people, you will be dehydrated and you will not get an adequate amount of exercise. You may have trouble sleeping or staying awake. The effect of these common symptoms of grief is to feel exhausted.

It helps to know that fatigue is a normal part of grief recovery. You may want to add this statement to the growing list of helpful reminders you post around your house: *Grief is heavy. To feel tired is normal. My fatigue too will not last forever.*

Grief recovery is hard work that requires a maximum of stamina and patience from you. Whatever else you call your movement through grief, you will surely label it an endurance contest of the first order.

Your Physical Health

Your health risk can be much higher after a major loss. The classic study done by Erich Lindemann in 1944 indicated the risk of coronary disease is 250 percent higher after the death of a spouse. Similarly higher risk factors emerged for cancer, high blood pressure, arthritis, diabetes, thyroid disease and skin disease.

Subsequent studies, including those of Dr. Glen Davidson at Southern Illinois University, indicate an increased risk for migraine headaches, chronic depression, low-back pain and blood-chemistry disorders. There is also an increased risk for alcohol and drug dependency.

The good news is your response to the grief that follows a major loss is not out of your control. You do not have to become a victim of health problems.

Things to do to take
care of yourself physically

Dr. Glen Davidson recommends the following five things to strengthen yourself for the work of grief recovery. In looking at more than 100 factors, only these five were found to make a measurable difference in protecting your health. The sooner you begin the better.

1. Be part of a support group. There is nothing more important for your physical health than having a group of people to talk to about the things you are experiencing. Where people who have all experienced some common loss gather, there is a "built-in" healing power. The single most common complaint I have heard from bereaved persons is the difficulty in finding someone who will listen with compassion to the stories of their losses. You can be assured that your need to talk about your loss will far

exceed the willingness of most family members and friends to listen.

A grief support group does not require high-skilled professional leadership to be effective. Appendix C provides instructions for 12 sessions. This plan has worked successfully for many people and it will also work for you.

2. Drink an adequate amount of water. Under the stress and emotional upheaval of grief, you will tend to be dehydrated without being aware of it. Over the length of time required for recovery, this dehydration can weaken your immune system.

The best plan is to drink two quarts of water per day. It may sound like a large quantity, but it works. I encourage people to fill two one-quart jars with water and place them in the refrigerator. For some people, it helps to add a slice of lemon. Then be sure to drink both of them before the day is over.

It is important to note that soft drinks (regular or diet), iced tea, coffee and alcoholic beverages are not substitutes for water. In fact, these can work against you, requiring even more water intake.

3. Follow an adequate nutritional plan. While it may be challenging, it is important for you to maintain a healthy, well-balanced nutritional plan while you are struggling through grief. Avoid junk food, high-fat foods and excesses of sugar, caffeine and alcohol.

The challenge for most of us is that eating is a social occasion too. If you have to eat alone, food may have no interest to you during the early weeks and months after a major loss. It is common for people to put off eating until hunger reaches the point of discomfort, then overeat the wrong kinds of foods. The best rule-of-thumb is to try to maintain your weight within five pounds of what it was prior to your loss.

You will find a list of desirable foods and a sample menu in Appendix B of this book. If you have any physical problems, check with your doctor for suggested guidelines.

4. Get adequate exercise. Exercise, within the boundaries of your own limitations, is helpful both physically and emotionally. Forty-five minutes of brisk walking can do wonders for relieving the symptoms of depression—and it's free! Stretching, swimming and whatever level of aerobic exercise your doctor permits can all be of great benefit to you.

You will tend to be more regular in exercising if you get someone else to do it with you. The most difficult part of any exercise program is getting to it when you don't feel like it. Most of the time you will feel better and have more energy when you are finished. Having a friend who will help you keep making the decision to do your exercising is a great help.

5. Get sufficient rest. There is no substitute for getting enough rest while dealing with grief. It is good if you can stay as close as possible to the sleeping pattern you had before your loss. Because of the fatigue and stress, it is even better to add additional resting time in the form of naps for the first several months after your loss.

Sleep disturbance is very common after any major loss. On pages 157-58 you will find instructions for things to do to help you stabilize your sleeping patterns. It includes a detailed plan to follow if you wake up in the middle of the night and can't get back to sleep.

Developing Grief Fitness

Working through grief is a little like working out for physical fitness. Those who lift weights cannot start with the maximum weight they hope to lift. Those who jog or walk can't begin with a maximum distance. They have to work up to these goals a little at a time.

In the same way, you don't start out handling grief the

way you will later on. You must grow in your grief fitness a little at a time. It doesn't come easily. But it is the way to regain your balance in life after a major loss.

Over and over again you will need to tell yourself, "I will not always feel as I do now." You will need patience with others and with yourself. You need to remember that sometimes you will feel worse before you feel better.

It isn't uncommon during the first year or two to have times when you think the work is finished. And then something happens to plunge you back into the depths of anguish.

The first year after a death or divorce is dominated by constant reminders. Almost every week brings another *first time without* experience. The first birthday, anniversary, Christmas, Jewish holy days and other special dates are often terribly painful.

It may come down to enduring one more night of loneliness or one more meal across from an empty chair. It helps to know the first year after a major loss is not going to be one of the best years in your life. But it doesn't have to be the worst year either. It has a purpose and a direction. You can come to the end of the year and know you have made a significant accomplishment just because you survived.

Passing the anniversary date of a major loss can be like a graduation day. People say to me, "I didn't think I could do it, but I did." I see a new spark in their eyes. They have endured the worst and survived. You, too, can do that.

The Lonely Year

The second year of grief calls for more patience with yourself than with anyone else. After getting through the first year, you may think life will return to normal. It doesn't. Many bereaved people call the second year of grief their *lonely year*. They say that surviving the first year proves you will make it. The second year proves how lonely it can be to make it without the one you lost.

It may seem as if you are starting all over again. You aren't. This is a good time to join a grief support group or to rejoin if you dropped out.

Once the second-year crisis is past, you will be ready to start getting on with the reorganization of your life after loss. This doesn't mean there is no more grieving to do. It means you will have developed sufficient skills to handle your grief.

In time and with hard work, the good days will begin to outnumber the bad ones. By the end of the third year, the pain of your loss should be diminished to the point where it finally seems manageable.

Perhaps the most important growth that will come to you during grief recovery is the sense of confidence and pride that emerges. You have endured the very worst of all experiences and finished on top. You are a different person, a stronger person and a better person than when you started.

10

The Use and Abuse
of Religion

Beliefs that help or hurt

M Y WIFE AND I DID NOT GROW UP with a religious faith. Our families did not attend church when we were children and by the time we reached adolescence neither of us had any interest in attending. We were not anti-religion. We really had no feelings about it at all.

Shortly after our marriage, my wife's six-year-old brother was killed in an automobile accident. We were away on a weekend camping trip and returned to find a neighbor waiting to break the tragic news to us. As waves of shock and disbelief rolled over us, we cried out, "Oh God, please don't let it be!"

The fact that we were not church-going people didn't matter, nor did our almost total ignorance of the Bible and prayer. In the moment we were up against a tragedy, the word "God" was foremost in our vocabulary.

In the months that followed, we blamed God for Ronnie's death. We promised ourselves never to care about anyone so much again because God was so cruel. In our darkest times we denied there was a God. We may have been disinterested in spiritual matters before our loss, but when confronted with death and grief, God was at the center of our thoughts and conversation.

Our experience is a common one. Talking about the role of God and religion in times of major loss is almost universal.

❖ *"I lost my faith in God when I had a miscarriage."*

❖ *"My faith is all that held me together when we divorced."*

❖ *"Why did God take my husband from me?"*

❖ *"How can God allow someone who was so kind to suffer so much?"*

❖ *"Knowing my child is with God gives me the courage to go on."*

These statements come from people who experienced a major loss. They reflect the kinds of thoughts that are common when life seems to come crashing down around us.

A Help or a Hindrance?

In the weeks, months and years following a major loss, religious faith continues to have a major impact on grief recovery. The question is: Will your faith have a positive impact or a negative impact?

Will your spiritual-religious orientation *help* you cope with a major loss (or series of losses)? Will the things you believe about God help as you go through the process of grief and try to recover a sense of joy, or will your religious beliefs *hinder* your coping ability? Will your view of faith get in the way of a healthy, effective grief recovery?

The best answer to each of these questions is: It all depends on what you believe and how you practice your beliefs.

When the news of Ronnie's death reached us, my wife and I were ill-prepared to cope with such a tragic event. Life itself seemed to come crashing down around us. The image I had was of falling into a dark, musty well with no bottom. I saw us tumbling deeper and deeper into hopelessness and despair.

It wasn't any easier on Susan whose husband of 24 years took her to their favorite restaurant for dinner on Christmas Eve—and over dessert announced he was divorcing her to be with someone else.

You know the kinds of experiences I'm describing.

❖ *The doctor says, "You have cancer."*

❖ *Your paycheck comes with a piece of pink paper attached to it.*

❖ *Millions of people every year now receive the dreaded news: HIV positive.*

❖ *The telephone rings in the night and you know before you pick it up that a loved one has died.*

Religion can be a tremendous resource at such times. It can provide incredible strength for walking the pathway of grief recovery. Dr. Howard Clinebell, an internationally recognized authority on grief and loss, says a healthy religious faith and the support of a spiritual community have a unique ability to help us turn *miserable minuses* into *positive pluses*. In her book, *Living Through Personal Crisis*, Ann Kaiser Stearns says, "Faith is a powerful energy when it represents the trust that, with struggle, our sorrows can be overcome." [1]

Religious faith can also get in the way of recovery. It can, in fact, be an almost insurmountable barrier to healing the deep wounds of grief.

Whether your religion is a help or a hindrance depends upon whether you use it in ways that are appropriate and healthy, or abuse it through beliefs that are unhealthy and inappropriate. This can happen when we look for short, simple answers to complex questions for which there are no simple answers or look for "magical" ways to either bypass grief or resolve it quickly.

If you look upon religious faith as an inoculation against the kinds of tragedies you see happening to others, you will be poorly prepared when tragedy happens to *you*. If you see your faith as a "quick-fix" for sadness, you will be ill-prepared to cope with an emotional wound that, under the best of circumstances, can take two to three years to heal. If you think that believers should handle grief more easily than non-believers, your "faith" will be a barrier to your recovery.

The abuse of religion also makes it next to impossible to resolve the ever-present questions of "why?" when a major loss occurs.

Beliefs that Hurt

Jimmy had been a problem to his family during his teenage years. He was wild, did foolish things that often resulted in injuries to himself including using several kinds of illegal drugs. Throughout all of his escapades, he avoided any permanent injury and never was in serious trouble with the law. By the time he reached young adulthood, he began to settle down. He married, moved out of the state, away from the influences in his life over which he seemed to have little control. In the fullest sense, he made a new start.

This included a job at which he did well and the birth of a child. His parents finally were able to heave a sigh of relief that their son was leading a useful and happy life.

One day the telephone rang. It was their daughter-in-law, telling them through her tears that Jimmy had been killed in an industrial accident. The question "why?" dominated his parents' thoughts for the next two years.

There were those, including the minister who offici-ated at Jimmy's funeral, who suggested his death was God's will and should not be questioned. Some inferred that Jimmy had put his life right with God and thereby "qualified" for being taken to heaven. The grief recovery of Jimmy's parents was severely inhibited by such abuses of religion.

When our daughter was in high school, we lived in a small community. The school received good support from the town for its athletic programs. There was a tightly knit sense of unity between the students, teachers and parents.

Our daughter, along with six other girls, was a song leader who performed at football games and parades. During her senior year, one of the other song leaders was killed in a car accident. Her boyfriend was driving. In a moment of carelessness he lost control and the car rolled, throwing Jan out and crushing her.

The funeral was held in the town's only mortuary. The service was packed to overflowing with grieving students, parents, teachers and community leaders. Everyone was in shock. As we arrived, we passed small groups of teen-agers huddled together, sobbing uncontrollably as they tried to console one another. Again and again I heard young voices ask why God would allow such a thing like this to happen?

As the service started, more than 200 pairs of tear-filled eyes were looking hopefully at the young minister who was in charge. When he began his sermon I began to get sick in the pit of my stomach.

He began by telling those grief-stricken people that Jan's death was a blessing. He said God was out walking in the heavenly garden and looked for the most beautiful flower to pick. Jan was chosen. He praised the young man whose carelessness had caused her death for having such faith that he could smile and rejoice that Jan was in heaven.

I wanted to stand up and scream "NO!" I probably would have made matters worse if it hadn't been for my more-in-control wife. She placed her hand on top of my white knuckles gripping the seat in front of me and quietly said, "Not now. It isn't the time." She was right. Perhaps this book is the time.

Some of those young people left that place thinking they should not be too good or they might be next on God's flower list. Others were encouraged to bury their grief and anger where it could become distorted and hurtful. The young man who had driven the car went on "praising the Lord" until the day he collapsed and had to have extensive psychiatric treatment.

This event remains for me the classic example of the abuse of religion as a resource for grief recovery.

Answering the Question "Why?"

"Why?" questions are a normal part of the grief recovery process, but they are just one step along the way. Recovery depends upon, among other things, letting go of the "why?" questions and turning instead to questions that begin with the word "how."

The hard fact is: When we experience a major loss there is no satisfactory answer to the question "Why?"— unless we are ready to say that this is a mortal, frail world that is full of flaws. It isn't perfect and life doesn't follow a perfect script. It's a world on which we can depend for nothing except the certainty of suffering. Whatever our religious orientation may be, the message is the same: Experiencing major loss is not optional.

Ours is a physical world in which the laws of gravity and physics operate. Therefore, accidents do happen.

The world is also a place where human beings have a freedom of will that can be used for destructive purposes as much as for constructive ones. A young single parent moved to our community to get away from the problems of Chicago's inner city. She had been in her new apartment only a few weeks when she stepped outside to take her baby for a walk. A neighbor, who reported he didn't like the music she played, waited until she was in the open, then shot and killed her.

Read your newspaper or watch the television news. This is a mortal, frail, imperfect world in which tragedies not only can occur, they do. And, religious people are no more immune to these tragedies than anyone else. There is not some grand plan or purpose to every major loss event we experience. Trying to find meaning and reason in such events is childish because there is no acceptable explanation. It can also harm the grief recovery of those who are most involved.

Progressing to "How?" Questions

To ask "why?" when a major loss happens is certainly normal, but a vital sign of recovery is the emergence of questions beginning with the word "how." "How can I work through this loss and achieve as full a life as possible?" "How can I use this experience to help someone else?" "How do I find meaning in life alone after many years of marriage?" "How do I start a new career after being laid off?" "How can I be an effective parent now that I am divorced?" "How do I reenter the church as a single person after all this time as a couple?"

Questions beginning with the word "how" begin with an acknowledgment of the loss that has taken place. They carry with them the unspoken affirmation: *"I will survive this loss. I will live."*

A healthy religious faith, used in an appropriate way, can be a powerful resource for moving from questions of "why?" to those of "how?"

Beliefs that Help

Dell and Liz were active lay persons in their church. They held leadership positions that gave both of them high visibility. They were prominent in their community and well known to a wide circle of acquaintances. Everyone thought of them as warm, caring people. It was a total shock when Dell and Liz filed for divorce.

A part of the agony each of them felt was the sense that they were betraying their church, parents and friends. "Why is this happening to me?" was foremost in the minds of each of them. At first they made an effort to remain in the membership of the same church. It was a large congregation with multiple worship services on Sundays. It seemed possible that they could coexist comfortably, but it was not to be.

Questions emerged for both Dell and Liz: "How can I put my life back together?" "How can we keep from hurting others through our pain?"

Dell dropped out of the church, but immediately transferred his membership to another church of the same denomination.

During the course of their divorce, neither Dell nor Liz blamed God or the church for their struggles. As they searched their own minds and hearts, they both found their faith in God's love and acceptance to be a source of hope. Church friends rallied around both of them with concern and assurances of continuing support.

In time, Dell remarried and is again a leader in his new church. Liz not only stayed in her church, she became the leader in organizing a singles program. Even when she remarried, her interest in the singles program remained high. She encouraged the church to establish a regular position of Singles Coordinator and arranged a network of people who are on call to newly divorcing people. The church now has social programs for singles as an alternative to staying home alone or making the rounds of singles bars.

Out of one couple's very real grief experience has emerged a many-faceted program of support and healing for others. The faith of Dell and Liz was able to encompass something as painful and embarrassing to them as divorce. The congregation was willing to enter into their loss and grieve with them without being judgmental.

Because of everyone's use of religious faith, something very good came out of a tragic loss.

Four Ways Religion Helps

There are four very distinct, precise ways that a healthy religious faith, used appropriately, can be of tremendous help at a time of major loss.

Religion influences one's fundamental view of life

There are two fundamentally different points of view from which to begin the task of grief recovery: For the non-believer, life is temporary and death is permanent. For the believer, death is temporary and life is permanent. These statements represent vastly different starting points for the task of grief recovery. The task to be done is the same for both, but the underlying belief system is quite different.

For the non-believer, death is the great *Canceled Stamp* on every achievement. One may have achieved many good things in life, but all that is canceled by death.

To see life as temporary and death as permanent is to live by the motto, "It was nice while it lasted, but it's all over now."

The permanency of death gives greater power to all the other losses in life. A beer advertisement proclaimed: "You only go around once in life, so grab for all the gusto you can get." The implication is we must get it now for there is no tomorrow. So, what if I invest all my life in a career—and get laid off? What if the marriage I meant to be forever ends in divorce? How do I face the inevitable decline in my physical strength that comes with age? How do I begin the process of grieving for my lost loved one?

I know there are answers to questions such as these, but I don't know what those answers are. I see non-believing people recover from major losses.

I believe life is permanent and death is temporary. This does not in any way diminish the pain I feel when a loved one dies or make major losses any less real.

However, for any believer, the starting point of grief recovery is different. Death, instead of being the great Canceled Stamp, is the ultimate nuisance. Death can interrupt the best laid plans of those married 60 years or more, but it can cancel nothing. The believer looks at the experience of grieving as a dark valley through which to walk, just as the non-believer does. But for the believer the dark valley is not a box canyon. It is something through which to travel to get to a destination on the other side.

I remind every couple who comes to me for premarital counseling that every marriage ends in one of two ways, death or divorce. I know of no other options. It helps to give newlyweds a realistic frame of reference for all of their planning and relating.

Perhaps the best definition of death I have heard is this: "Death is that thing that happens when we are busy making other plans."

Death can work havoc in our lives, but according to my faith system, neither death nor any other major loss has the power to cancel anything. I said that to a group of single parents and was asked, "What about divorce?" One lady said, "Those who lose their husbands to death are lucky. They can at least go to a grave and express their mourning and pray for the deceased. In my case, he is still walking around after our divorce and I only *wish* he were dead!" But even *that* woman had to admit that not all of her former marriage was bad. There had been moments of intimacy and special times that were wonderful. The divorce did not have the power to cancel out those experiences unless she allowed it to.

My wife and I meet with 30 or more persons every week in a grief support group. Most are widowed, some have lost children and a few have spouses with Alzheimer's disease. These folks are able to express deep love and sentiment for their loved ones, even years after the person's death. They are able to relive precious moments and shed tears freely as we talk about the life they shared together. The dominant emotion, through tears and all, is that of joy. They know it isn't over—it's just interrupted.

Religious faith can provide the motivation required for grief recovery

There is a very heavy weight to grief—and the process of recovery calls for a lengthy wait. Grief is fatiguing. It wears you down. The indescribable anguish can rip and tear at your insides, making little responsibilities seem overwhelming. Sometimes just remembering a name or your telephone number is impossible.

When anguish pummels your feelings to the point of numbness, there is still the oppressive, silent sadness that just leans on you without ever seeming to let up. Under this kind of pressure, we need something to motivate us to take the first steps toward recovery. If the journey of a thousand miles begins with the first step, the first step on the path to renewed joy and vitality after a major loss is the most difficult of all.

This is the place where a grief support group can be so important, but often taking the step to go to a group is extremely difficult. It is here that religious faith can play a major role.

Jewish and Christian scriptures provide vivid images to help us be motivated enough to take at least a baby step on the long road to recovery. The most familiar image is that found in the Psalms, "Yea, though I walk through the valley of the shadow of death, I will fear no evil." It's powerful imagery. It says that somebody has done it before. Nearly all newly bereaved people think they are the only ones to ever feel as they do. It also says that the path of grief is not a dead-end street, but a well-marked trail to a destination.

Religion is a great antidote for the loneliness that accompanies every major loss

The one factor of grief that is common to everyone, regardless of the kind of loss experienced, is loneliness.

"I am the only one who has ever felt this way."

"Nobody else can understand my grief."

"I am alone and I will always feel as I do right now."

To eat alone, watch a sunset alone, see some historic event on television alone or just have a passing thought with no one else to share it with can be a terrifying experience. The single most common complaint among widowed persons is: "My need to talk about my loss far exceeds the willingness of my family and friends to listen to me."

Those in the Christian tradition tell me there is great comfort in the words attributed to Jesus at the close of the Gospel of Matthew: "Remember, I am with you until the end of the age." I would translate those words to say,

"Loneliness is always an illusion. It means that if everyone else deserts me, I am not alone." That belief has held me together more than once in a time of personal loss. It doesn't make the pain of our losses any less, but it can make them bearable.

Your religious community can provide supportive strength

Never underestimate the supportive power of a religious community (church, synagogue or fellowship). For all the failings of people in our churches and synagogues, there are no other groups who do so much at a time of major loss.

Funerals or memorial services held in the familiar surroundings of the bereaved person's regular place of worship offer a warmth not found in mortuary chapels. The simple act of providing food and a reception following the service — or taking food to the home — brings a sense of belonging and the assurance of being loved.

Ministers, priests and rabbis are the only professionally trained persons in our society who do not need an invitation to reach out to people at a time of any major loss. Many times someone in our congregation has asked me to visit a neighbor or friend who has lost a loved one to death or gone through a divorce. In most cases, these are not people who have attended our church. They did not call to request my involvement, they just shared their sorrow with a neighbor or friend. I have never been refused entrance to a home when I have called. A doctor cannot do that and neither can a psychologist or social worker. It is a rare privilege given to religious leaders, and with the privilege comes responsibility.

For all the religious community does, there is so much more that can be done. Traditionally, congregations have been directly involved in supportive ways with bereaved people for about one week. With all that is now known about the length of a normal grief recovery, it is imperative that congregations be involved for a minimum of three years. No other group in society is in such an advantageous place to be with people for the long haul. Providing grief support groups and divorce recovery groups, making contact on the anniversary of a death and providing one-on-one contact to make reentry into church worship and activities easier are all ways that churches and synagogues help people through grief.

In our congregation, one of the ministers visits the widowed person on the anniversary of the spouse's death, taking a plant or flower arrangement. It is a visible way to say, "We understand your grief and we are ready to continue caring about you."

Survivors are often challenged by some household responsibility that was carried out by the one who is now deceased. We keep a list of persons with special skills in the most common areas, such as accounting, plumbing, electrical, automotive maintenance, cooking and driving a car. When a need is expressed, a referral is made to one of the volunteers who provides the needed assistance.

Other churches have provided "shepherds" or other caregivers, who are available to initiate contact on a regular basis to offer a listening ear. This has proven especially helpful to divorcing persons in addition to those who have lost a spouse or child to death.

In all of these ways a healthy religious faith and a sensitive religious community can be of tremendous help in a time of major loss.

What Religion Cannot Do

There are only three things that religious faith cannot do for us. Understanding and accepting these limitations is as important for grief recovery as utilizing the things that faith does so well.

Religious faith cannot give us
immunity from loss

Practicing "fire insurance" religion (reading the Bible, attending services, tithing, praying and doing good deeds for the primary purpose of avoiding divine punishment) leaves folks ill-prepared to cope with the losses that are an inherent part of being a real person in this mortal world. Being persons of faith does not excuse us from our own mortality or that of our loved ones.

Those who pretend that the "rules" of life are different for people of faith face an almost certain sense of guilt when something goes wrong. We hear this point of view in such statements as, "I wonder what he/she did to deserve that?" or, "Somebody up there was sure looking out for you this time." I hear bereaved survivors questioning how God could allow their loved one to die when he/she "was such a good person who was loved so much."

It's of vital importance to grief recovery that we understand that death, divorce and other major losses are not necessarily deserved or the result of God taking time out from looking after us. The rain still falls on the good and not-so-good alike. Good fortune seems to pour out on people without much regard to their morals or religious character—and so do major losses.

In the early days of our religious experience, my wife and I belonged to a prayer group. We not only met to pray for ourselves, but often members of the group would visit sick people in their homes or in the hospital. A request came for the group to pray for a woman who was diagnosed with inoperable cancer. A tumor in her abdomen was the size of a grapefruit. She was given no chance for survival. Three members of the prayer group went to her home and prayed for her.

Upon her next visit to the doctor, the examination showed the tumor was gone. Needless to say there was joyful celebration, not only in her household, but among members of the prayer group. They were sure God had intervened in response to their prayers and faithfulness. A month later, the woman died of a heart attack.

More recently, my wife and I were driving to a meeting at 2:30 p.m. on a clear, sunny Sunday afternoon. As we approached an intersection, the light was green and all traffic was stopped. The intersection was empty of vehicles. As we slowed, then proceeded through, we never saw the car that ran the red light and hit us broadside. Police estimated it was traveling at least 45 miles per hour at impact. Our car was totaled, but we escaped with only moderate injuries.

The response of some church members was, "This can't happen to you, we can't get along without you." Others said, "God was sure looking out for you." A few days later, four teenagers were killed when their car went out of control and hit a light pole a few blocks away from the scene of our accident.

If we survived our accident because God was looking out for us, does that mean God decided not to care about those young people? If the woman the prayer group prayed for recovered from cancer because of their prayers, does it mean they failed to pray adequately for her heart? Or, does God "draw straws" to see when we win or lose?

It seems to me to make much more sense and to be much more in harmony with the basic tenets of our Judeo-Christian heritage to say, "This is a mortal, imperfect, frail and flawed world. Life is not always fair. Tragedy and major loss are as much a part of life as victory and times of joy. As a human being, I am subject to these realities. So are my loved ones. My one and only assurance from God is that I will never be deserted in any circumstance."

Such a perspective may not be comfortable, but it is real and it provides a solid foundation for utilizing faith in the most helpful way at the time of a major loss.

Religious faith cannot give us back
our dead loved ones or our dead relationships

The one thing bereaved persons want more than anything else is to have their loved ones returned to them. It is the one thing that neither we nor God can give them.

Strange as it may seem, to acknowledge this fact up front with a survivor is always comforting. It says that we understand the enormity of the loss and lets the bereaved person know that we have no simple or pat answers. What every person needs in the face of a major loss is compassion, understanding, a listening ear and a willingness to carry out needed tasks without being asked. To down-play the pain of a death or divorce with religious platitudes frequently only magnifies the sense of loss.

For the caregiver to acknowledge the finality of the loss is often the beginning of the journey to recovery for the survivor. Loss means gone forever, at least for the duration of this life. The mechanism of denial is overcome when the survivor understands *and acts* on this excruciatingly painful reality. It is at this point that the most basic decision of recovery can be made—"I will live!" That decision will have to be renewed many times throughout the first year of recovery.

To acknowledge that our religious faith cannot bring back our dead loved ones is in no way a denial of life after death. I have no doubt that my friends and family members who have died are "okay" in God's eternal heaven. While that affirmation gives me a certain sense of comfort *for them*, it does not diminish my sadness or loneliness at losing them. Whatever else their condition is, one thing is clear: I will not see them again in this life. This part of my history is ended.

Frequently, people have been told that their loved ones were in a bettter place and they would one day be reunited with them. When this kind of thing is said in a way that implies the bereaved person's grief should therefore be lessened, it becomes very hurtful. It can even inhibit grief recovery and increase the health risk of the bereaved person.

We must understand that loss = gone and gone = forever. The possibility for a full and rewarding life after any loss begins here.

Religious faith cannot provide a shortcut through grief

Every clergyperson I know wishes this were not true. We would give anything to find a pathway of faith that would take people from the point of their losses to a full recovery—and do it quickly. Unfortunately, there doesn't seem to be such a shortcut available to us.

It is another of those strange-but-true facts of grief recovery that religious faith serves us best when we start out understanding that the pain of grief will not be less nor will the path to recovery be shorter because of our religion.

Again, for the sake of the physical health of bereaved persons if nothing else, clergy and laity must never let people think that if they have prayed for them, their grief should be lessened. People who maintain a classic "stiff upper lip" and who come back to church without tears should not be publicly praised or held up as the ideal of faith. More often than not, those who are having the worst time—who weep uncontrollably and seem to need the most help, are actually doing the best job of grieving.

Trying to shortcut the grief process is like giving someone with hypoglycemia a major dose of sugar. The person might feel quite high—for a little while, but an even greater crash will follow.

What the divorcing and the bereaved need from their pastors and congregations is the assurance that their church will not desert them over the long haul of grief recovery. Providing support groups, special programs dealing with losses, a bereavement care team and making the effort to *initiate* contact with those who have suffered a major loss for at least two years (three is better), are all ways the church can say, "We know this is a long, tough and painful journey for you. We want you to know that we will be with you every step of the way."

Religion and You

Religion and the religious community can be tremendous resources for you in times of major loss. But, you must understand that loss and grief are a part of life for the believer and unbeliever alike. All of us are subject to disappointment, heartbreak and death. When you have a major loss it will hurt regardless of your faith or lack of faith.

You will search for hope. The hope that will serve you best acknowledges life will never be the same again—but insists that life after loss can still be full and good. The resources of religious faith can be strong motivators to reach for this hope. If you believe God has been present with human losses for a long time, you will be encouraged to try again when you want to quit. You will be able to accept new places, new stages of life. You will know that whatever challenges you face now, or in some future loss, you will not face them alone.

[1] Ann Kaiser Stearns. *Living Through Personal Crisis*. New York: Ballantine, 1984.

11

Children
and Grief

It's a big hurt for little people too

TRY TO IMAGINE WHAT IT IS LIKE to experience the death of a loved one, the break-up of your family or any other major loss as a child.

❖ *You have all of the sadness, fear, anger and other emotions that adults have.*

❖ *You do not have the vocabulary to express the way you are feeling.*

❖ *Your limited exposure to life leaves you with little understanding of what is happening to you.*

❖ *You probably assume you were to blame in some way.*

If you can imagine these circumstances, you have some idea of how children grieve.

When someone dies, children feel the loss as much as any adult. They just don't have the words to tell us about their feelings.

When adults try to shelter and protect them from the experience, children turn to their own imaginations that often produce a worse situation than the real one. Young children often assume they are somehow to blame for the loss. They are used to thinking in terms of blame for spilled drinks and broken toys. It's easy for children to interpret the combination of adult silence and sadness as disappointment in *them*. If a parent or grandparent dies, the child may think that all adults in his or her life will die. If parents divorce, children may think it is they who are no longer loved.

Perhaps the most important thing for adults to understand is the crucial role we play in the future lives of children after a major loss in their lives. When the adults respond in ways that help the child face loss and work through grief just as we must do, there are no lasting emotional scars. When adults fail to respond in helpful ways, the effects are often seen for the rest of the child's life. Among these effects is the continuation of the problem to another generation. The child who carries grief wounds into adulthood will tend to be uncaring and unhelpful to others in times of grief.

Matthew and Lisa were six and eight years old respectively when their mother put them in the kitchen with bowls of cereal, went into the family den and shot herself. The children found her body and called neighbors for help.

The children's father was wise enough to take them to a skilled counselor. She sat on the floor with Matthew and Lisa, helping them draw pictures of their mommy. Some of their pictures reflected their child's anger at mom for leaving them. Others showed the fear they were feeling. Others depicted better times when mom was happy.

On the day of the funeral, Matthew and Lisa placed some of their drawings in the casket with the body of their mother. Each of them added a small gift they had chosen.

Over the next several months, the counselor helped them understand that mother did not die because she was angry at them. She assured them her death had nothing to do with their failure to pick up clothes or toys. It wasn't because they had been naughty or hadn't eaten everything on their plates at dinner. Mom was very sad down inside. She loved them and didn't mean to make them sad. Her death was a tragic event that she couldn't help.

Sunday school teachers in Matthew and Lisa's church were instructed to be prepared to listen to them carefully and to be sure they understood it was not God's will for their mother to die.

In time, their father remarried. Matthew and Lisa are happy in their new home. They love their stepmother, who makes sure they remember their "real" mother on special occasions. They will be okay.

When the adults in a child's life do not respond in appropriate ways, the results can be quite different than Matthew and Lisa's experience.

Rosemary was about the same age as Matthew and Lisa when her life was turned upside down. Her father, who suffered from chronic depression, was successful in taking his own life on the fourth attempt. Unfortunately for Rosemary the adults in her life did not respond in a healthy way as happened with Matthew and Lisa.

Her mother became addicted to alcohol and drugs, withdrew from the support of family, friends and church and "went off the deep end." She entered into multiple sexual relationships and worked only sporadically. Rosemary reverted to bed-wetting, lost weight and couldn't sleep. She seemed frightened and insecure.

The probability is high that Rosemary has suffered emotional scars that will permanently damage the quality of her life.

Telling Children about Death

To provide the opportunity for healing that children need after a death, adults can do the following five things:

1. Provide an open and honest atmosphere in which it is easy for children to ask questions and express their own thoughts and feelings. This includes involving children in family discussions about the person, the death and funeral plans. It may be important to sit down on the floor while talking with younger children. Holding them on your lap and giving frequent assurances of their security and your love for them can ease many fears. Remember: While adults internalize feelings, children act them out. Watch for signs of the need for your attention.

2. Understand how children are interpreting their experience with death. I find asking children specific questions enables them to tell me what they are thinking and feeling. I ask such things as:

❖ *Have you ever been to a funeral? What was it like?*

❖ *Have you ever seen or touched a dead person?*

❖ *What do you think you will see at the funeral?*

❖ *What else do you know about death and funerals?*

❖ *What would you like to know?*

❖ *What would you like to ask* _____ *(name of the deceased person)?*

The fact that you are willing to talk matter-of-factly about these things is very reassuring to children. It is helpful if you sit on the floor or at a low table and provide paper and crayons, a coloring book or modeling clay to enable children to express themselves.

3. Give correct and factual information in as simple a way as you can. Dispel myths and the creations of the child's imagination. Do not use phrases such as "Grandpa has gone away, Mommy is sleeping" or "God wanted him." Younger children take your words as literal, absolute fact. To say someone has "gone away" may be interpreted by children to mean the deceased person wanted to leave them. If you say the person is "sleeping," they will wait for him or her to wake up. I have heard more than one child say fearfully that if God wanted someone else, God may want me next.

A useful and helpful statement to a young child (under the age of seven) would be something like this:

> *When someone dies, it means their body is no longer working. Their heart stops beating and they don't breathe any more. They don't have to eat or sleep. They are never too cold or too hot. Nothing hurts. They don't need their body anymore and that means we won't see them.*

This statement will have to be repeated many times on subsequent occasions because death is not perceived to be a permanent condition by young children.

When her 12-year-old brother was killed, Dawn, aged three, alternately understood that he was gone and expected to see him again. Michael's body was cremated and taken by the family to another state for burial. Dawn saw ashes in an ashtray at the airport and thought it was Michael. When the plane began its descent, Dawn began to cry thinking the plane would land on Michael. When they disembarked, she was disappointed he wasn't there to meet them.

Each time the child expresses confusion, you need to repeat the same statement in the same way. Begin by saying, "Remember (name) has died, and when someone dies, it means...

4. Help children preview what will happen at a viewing, memorial or funeral service. Describe the physical setting and what the child will see. If possible, show the child a picture of a casket. Describe what the body will look like. If any marks or wounds will be visible, describe them as simply as you can.

One of the most frequently asked questions is, "Should children be allowed to touch the body of the deceased?" The answer is, yes, if they want to and are prepared ahead of time. Children are naturally curious. How something feels is one way they determine if it is safe for them. Try to describe the feel of the body in terms the child can understand. Tell them the person will feel cool instead of warm. Have the child touch your arm and compare the feeling to touching the arm of a vinyl or leather-covered chair. A typical statement to make would go something like this:

You may touch (name) if you want to. However, now that his (or her) body is no longer working, it will feel different. Instead of being warm and soft, it will feel cool and sort of hard. It won't hurt (name) if you touch him (her) and it won't hurt you.

There are many horror stories about children having severe emotional damage done by touching or kissing a dead body. I have never encountered such a reaction nor has anyone else in my acquaintance who works with death and loss. Such fears seem to reflect more of an adult anxiety about death. The key to all of children's experience with death rests with the reaction and response of the adults around them.

5. Provide some means for children to say good-bye. The easiest and one of the most effective ways to do this

is to have the children draw a picture that can be placed in the casket. Be sure to make a copy for the child to keep. If children are old enough, they can write notes which are also placed in the casket. Other useful expressions are photographs, especially of the child with the deceased person, cassette-taped messages, toys or articles of clothing.

It is perfectly okay for children to see adults in tears. Just explain that you miss the deceased person too and feel very sad.

Age Makes a Difference

Children grieve and express their sadness in varying ways according to their age and development. It is not that young children do not grieve, they just perceive death and loss differently than adults or older children and respond differently. From infancy on, loss and grief are a normal part of human life.

Infancy

Infants show an understanding of loss well before their first birthday. They require physical touch and stroking for their development. Their two basic fears are loud noises and falling. Each of these is associated with a separation from the source of their security.

The first game many babies respond to is peek-a-boo. Interestingly enough, the name itself comes from the Old English and means, "alive or dead." First eye contact is made with the child, then some object is used to block the infant's view. Momentarily, the adult is gone as far as the infant is concerned. Then the object is removed and eye contact is reestablished accompanied by the words, "peek-a-boo." Frequently, this contact is reinforced by some physical touch.

A great moment comes in the life of every parent and grandparent when the infant is able to control the game by controlling the object which breaks the eye contact.

Preschool

Up through approximately age four, children sense loss and sadness, but cannot conceptualize death.

The fear of separation begins at about the age of one. After a death in the family, it is not uncommon for children to be afraid to be away from home or out of their parent's sight.

However, death does not seem permanent. It is more like taking a nap and waking up. The concept of time is limited. It may seem to a young child that death is only being less alive. With the exposure of most young children to many hours of television, this understanding is reinforced by seeing the same people "dead" on one program and alive a few days later.

Anita was four when her grandfather died. When she and her parents arrived at her grandparents' house, her grandfather's body was laid out in a casket in the front room. Anita was told that she must stay in the dining room. She peeked around the corner and saw a room full of adults standing around her grandfather's body. Several were crying because he was dead, but she didn't know what that meant. She wanted him to get up and play with her, but again was told she must stay in the other room.

On the day of the funeral, Anita was not allowed to attend the funeral, but was taken to the cemetery. When the casket lid was closed and it was lowered into the ground, she began to cry. She couldn't understand why they were all leaving grandpa alone in the ground. She thought he would be lonely and cold in the dark. She wondered if he had been bad and somebody was mad at him. When it was time to leave, she tried to tell her parents that her grandfather had not kissed her good-bye, but nobody was paying any attention.

Anita still carried the memory of this sad experience when she became a grandmother herself.

Elementary school

Between the ages of five and nine, the understanding of death becomes clear to most children. They come to realize that pets and people die and that death is final.

Jasmine had just celebrated her fifth birthday. She and her ten-year-old brother, Karl, were at home with their father while their mother was at work. The two children were ready for school and their father went out to start the car to take them. When Jasmine emerged from the house, her father was slumped over the wheel. She ran back inside to tell Karl that daddy was taking a nap in the car. Karl knew something was terribly wrong and called a neighbor for help.

Jasmine ran from person to person wanting to know when her daddy would take them on to school. Karl retreated to his room knowing their father was dead, but not knowing how to tell his sister the bad news.

At the funeral, Jasmine watched her father's body intently. At one point, she tugged on the sleeve of my wife's, dress and said, "I think I saw my daddy move. He's waking up now." June replied in a soft voice, "No, Jasmine, your father did not move. He is not sleeping, he is dead." Jasmine leaned against her, took June's hand and nodded in agreement. "Daddy's dead," she said.

Karl responded to his father's death in much the same way as the adult members of the family. His greatest worries were who would take care of them and would he have to leave school and go to work. Fortunately, Karl had adults around him who were willing to listen and to assure him that everything would work out in time.

Prepuberty and adolescence

By the time a child approaches adolescence, he or she has come a long way from the days of playing peek-a-boo. Death now has a social dimension in which concerns about the consequences will be paramount. The death of the same-sex parent when the child is about 12 or 13 years old seems to have the potential for lasting problems. It is wise to seek professional intervention when possible.

As adolescents move further into their teenage years, death raises philosophical questions about the meaning of life. It is a time when they feel immortal and death represents an intrusion of reality that can be terribly painful. If one of their peers dies, it represents a special challenge to their sense of security. If that death happened to be the result of suicide, professional intervention should be considered mandatory. Adolescents often become quite moody after a death, sometimes subjecting themselves to greater risks and impulsive behavior. Inviting teenagers to a grief support group or forming one just for them is quite appropriate.

General Guidelines for Adults

The most important insight adults can communicate to children of any age is that life goes on after a death, divorce or any major loss. To do this, you must become more comfortable with your own grief. The many exercises in this book can help you.

In addressing the needs of children of all ages at a time of loss, you will serve them well if you:

❖ *Offer your acceptance of their feelings and behavior.*

❖ *Listen carefully without being judgmental.*

❖ *Assure them of their security in terms they can understand.*

❖ *Make sure they understand they are not to blame.*

❖ *Express your love and care for them in unmistakable ways.*

❖ *Act in ways that elicit trust.*

❖ *Answer all questions with as much honesty as you can.*

❖ *Help them understand that circumstances will not always be the same and they will not always feel as they do now.*

❖ *Provide an atmosphere of stability in the midst of any changes.*

12

Making New Discoveries

Beginning with loss — ending with life

IT'S GREAT TO TALK with people who have made their way through grief! Those who have experienced a major loss and recovered from it remind me of explorers and adventurers.

Have you ever talked with a mountain climber or skydiver? Those who have conquered grief sound like people who have done such exciting and dangerous things. They will tell you not so much about what they have lost as about what they have *discovered*. Their lives will not be lived just in memories of the past, but also in new plans for the future.

If you have had a major loss recently, you probably can't imagine yourself thinking of anything else for the rest of your life. I assure you if you work through your grief in the ways I have been describing, you will not only think of new things, in time you will also sound like an adventurer.

Jean was a young wife with a two-year-old child. Her husband died suddenly after open-heart surgery. For the next three years Jean worked hard at her grief. She was a regular participant in our grief support group. Jean learned stress-reduction techniques and sought counseling for a nutrition plan to strengthen her body for the task. At every step along the way of her recovery, she refused to take the easy way out. In the midst of her own struggles she became one of our most dependable volunteers to visit newly bereaved people.

As she looks back now, Jean would tell you the experience has taught her she can do much more than she ever dreamed she could before Joe's death. Her family verifies she is indeed more confident and self-assured. She recently purchased a brightly colored hot-air balloon and is working towards her pilot's license, a dramatic symbol of the new life she has discovered after a terrible loss!

Jean would gladly give up her new self in exchange for having Joe back. But because getting her husband back is not possible, Jean is building a good life for her daughter and herself. She continues to discover brighter hopes with each new day.

Whereas Jean was a very outgoing person from the beginning, Alice was quiet and shy. She was a contented homemaker and mother of two sons until her husband got cancer. After his death Alice went through a very dark and dismal time that lasted for almost two years. Like Jean, she refused to give in to her grief or to run from it. Alice is convinced that Kleenex must have added an extra shift of workers to keep up with her need for tissues!

Today, three years after her loss, she works as a doctor's receptionist. She meets people easily, is considerably more forceful and dresses in brighter, bolder colors. Alice says, "It's hard to admit I'm a better person today, because it sounds like I'm glad Larry died. Nothing could be further from the truth. I'd give anything to have him back. But I do like the me that is emerging as a result of getting through my grief. I look back and I just can't believe I really did it."

Grief Is Ultimately about Making New Discoveries

Grief begins with a terrible and painful loss, but it can end with the discovery of new life. For all that is said in a negative way about grief, there is a positive side, too, if you will work through grief.

Jean and Alice each discovered a strength of character within themselves they had never known before. Each emerged with a new sense of pride and self-confidence. Each knows she was put to the ultimate test in life and was equal to the challenge. Neither of them ever wants to experience a major loss again, but both of them know deep inside that if it should happen, they can handle it. This discovery alone has added a new dimension of happiness and security to their lives.

You can make the same discovery. I believe each of us has a great deal more character than we think. But it often takes some major event in our lives to bring out that character.

Grief is not only a door-closer. Grief is also a door-opener. It's true that you cannot get back a loved one who has died or a part of your body lost to surgery. You aren't likely to get back a marriage that ended in divorce or a dream that was broken. It is equally true, however, that life can still be good for you. Once you have faced your grief squarely and taken the necessary steps to get directly through the center of it, you will see new sources of happiness that you couldn't see before.

When my father and mother died, I made a discovery that has continued to enriched my life from that time on. *I learned how to cry!* Before their deaths I had always handled my sorrow with stoic reserve. In working through my grief following their loss, I discovered I was actually healthier because I could cry. Tension and stress that were formerly stored in my neck and back were released through tears. My wife says I became a better husband. My children had a better father, my church a better minister.

In the ensuing years I have discovered that because I am free to cry, I am comfortable with the tears of others. This freedom has opened many new doors to helpful counseling. But I didn't learn the effectiveness of tears in a textbook. I learned it in the laboratory of my own loss and grief, and by allowing myself to be immersed in the grief experiences of others.

Attitude and Expectations Are Important

As uncomfortable as the thought may be, one grief experience does not give you immunity from future losses.

Dan and Dora had two sons. Their younger son died from a virus that caused an inflammation in his brain. Shortly after his death they moved, hoping the new environment would help them adjust to their loss. Sometime later, a daughter was born. Their surviving son, Michael, was 12 years old when he was kidnapped, sexually assaulted and brutally murdered. In the course of six years, these parents lost two of their three children.

Dan and Dora have taught me many priceless lessons about courage in the face of overwhelming grief. They, like Jean and Alice, did not try to sidestep the impact of their second tragedy. In the early going after Michael's death, they faced their grief under the bright light of media exposure.

Because Michael's body was abandoned in the desert

they were unable to see him after the tragedy. To experience the reality of what had happened, they asked the police to show them pictures taken at the murder scene. Later, they visited the site where it happened, several miles outside our city.

Pictures of Michael were left up in their home. Conversations about him were carried on daily. Because of local publicity, the man who killed their son was put on trial in another city 200 miles away. When the trial began, Dan and Dora were there. Throughout the trial and afterwards, they handled themselves with such openness and poise, they became inspirations to the entire community. A few months after Michael's death, a little girl in our city was abducted and killed. Among the first people to call the parents were Dan and Dora.

One of the most important things I learned from Dan and Dora was that working through the death of Kevin, their first son, helped prepare them for facing Michael's death. The most fundamental aspect of this preparation was they did not expect to be immune from tragedy.

Fortunately, not many of us have to face the kinds of tragedies Dan and Dora faced. But all of us need to remember that the very worst kind of loss is always *ours*.

If we expect to suffer for the rest of our lives after the death of a loved one, it will be difficult to let go and move on to new life. However, if we understand that the effective use of time will get us through grief, we have a foundation for getting at the work and beginning the process.

What you expect to discover after any loss plays an important role in your recovery from grief. The attitude with which you view the new possibilities that emerge for you is equally important.

I often hear statements like the ones that follow. The attitudes and expectations they represent are like stones blocking the doorway to new discoveries.

❖ *You never recover from a major loss such as death.*

❖ *Time is the only healer for grief.*

❖ *If you love someone too much your grief will be worse.*

❖ *Nobody else can help you with your grief.*

❖ *The death of a spouse is more painful than divorce.*

❖ *A slow death is easier to handle than a sudden death.*

❖ *Your loss was God's will and you should not question it.*

❖ *If you just keep busy, your grief will go away.*

Not one of those statements is true! Confronting loss and grief is one area of life where popular opinion is worth less than nothing. To build a new life after loss, you must understand the facts of loss even better than you understand the facts of life.

The following are true statements and represent important attitudes and expectations about loss and grief.

❖ *You can recover a full life after a major loss of any kind.*

❖ *It takes time to be healed from grief, and it also takes lots of hard work.*

❖ *The better your relationship with one who has died, the more satisfying your grief work will be.*

❖ *Many people can help you work through your loss, especially others who have had similar losses.*

❖ *Grief that results from divorce is similar in many ways to grief resulting from death and different in other ways. It is every bit as painful.*

❖ *It is never God's will for you to suffer nor for your loved ones to suffer or die. Death and loss are a part of this mortal life.*

❖ *If you keep too busy to face your feelings and avoid talking about them, you subject yourself to a higher risk of illness following a major loss.*

Viewing loss and grief in these ways will help you put your life together again. You can't avoid major losses. Important people, places and stages of life will be lost to you. Having one tragic loss doesn't mean you won't have others, but you can be assured your losses will open new doors as they close old ones.

13

Special Points
in Time

Mileposts on the road to recovery

CERTAIN POINTS IN TIME after a major loss are of
special significance. Chapter Four included a description
of the steps through grief that you can expect to take on
the way to recovery. The following are significant turning
points along your way. It helps to think of them as sign-
posts along the road, indicating you have come some
distance and are heading in the right direction. Each
represents a time of discovering something new and being
challenged to release a part of the past.

The Third Month

The third month after the death of a loved one or the filing of a divorce is often one of the most difficult times of all. By then all vestiges of shock and numbness are gone. The full impact of the loss is upon you.

Enough has happened by this time that denying your loss is impossible. If your spouse died, you have had three full months of filing insurance papers, death certificates and social-security forms. You have eaten and slept alone for 90 days. If your child died, you know by now that you aren't going to get your little one back. If you have divorced, your ex-spouse may already have a new love interest. The difficult adjustments of this step along the way to recovery will go on for some time. But for some reason, the third month will stand out in your mind as the most challenging.

Lori was 35 years old when her mother suddenly and unexpectedly died. They had lived in separate states since Lori and her husband moved away shortly after their marriage. The two women had maintained telephone contact over the years and greatly enjoyed catching up on each other's news each week.

Ninety days after her mother's death, Lori came to see me because she found her thoughts dominated by suicide. She was certain her mother had come to visit her the night before. Her message to Lori was one of loneliness for her and the wish that Lori could be with her.

In the brightness of day, Lori knew her suicidal impulses weren't rational. At night, she had more problems with them. I explained that what was happening was a normal phenomenon for the third month of her grief recovery. We set up a series of counseling sessions and a procedure for her to call if the night became too difficult.

After meeting several times, I suggested to Lori that she write a letter of good-bye to her mother. She was to tell her mother how much she loved her, how much she had enjoyed their years together and the special nature of their relationship. But now she had to let her go. Lori had to say good-bye so that she could go on with her life with her husband and family. She would miss her mother very much and would never forget her. She would show her gratitude for all her mother had taught her by living a new life with its own fulfillments. After writing the letter, Lori was to read it aloud several times each day until she could get through it without breaking down. Then she was to bring the letter and read it to me.

Lori was able to carry out that difficult task. It proved to be the key in enabling her to put away her self-destructive thoughts. As she faced the reality of her grief and understood more about what to expect of herself, Lori was able to move through it without further threat to herself.

Make a note on your calendar about three months after you experience any significant loss. When some sign of your reaction to it occurs that you didn't expect, you can check the date and say to yourself, "Oh, it's about three months since _____, I'm due for something like this." That simple exercise can turn your normal grief reaction into a time of discovery instead of panic.

If you are not already in some kind of a support group by the third month, try to find one. It is a time when talking with a professional counselor or clergyperson is better than the advice of inexperienced friends or family.

Six to Nine Months

This is a special time when you need to focus on the relationship of your body and emotions. Somewhere between six and nine months after a major loss, you could be quite vulnerable to the onset of a serious physical illness. Dr. Glen Davidson's study of bereaved persons indicated about 25 percent of them underwent a diminishing of their natural immune system during this period. I strongly urge marking your calendar at the fifth month also and scheduling a doctor's appointment for a physical.

Pat's husband died. His death forced her to close down a home for runaway youth and move to a new state to find work. She had to say good-bye to friends with whom she had a long and close relationship. Ten months later Pat developed a mysterious illness. She ran a high fever, suffered from exhaustion and became too weak to walk without support. Tests revealed an immune deficiency of an unknown classification. In time, the disease disappeared as mysteriously as it had appeared. Pat is convinced that the roots of this trying experience are in the grief she experienced as a result of her losses.

One Year

You don't need to mark the anniversary date of your loss on the calendar. Every widow or widower and every divorced person can tell you the date and hour their loss occurred. You will probably never forget the date of your loss either. The anniversary date of a loved one's death is particularly significant. You will have done something you thought was impossible a few months earlier. You will have survived an entire year without someone who was as important to you as life itself.

The anniversary date is often a mixture of sadness and hopefulness for many people. You are reminded in a vivid way of how much you have lost and how much it still hurts. But, you have come through the year and you are more hopeful for the next one.

After Lucy's husband died, those of us who knew her had a special concern. She didn't seem to be adjusting very well. She came to the grief support group a few times, then dropped out. She appeared to be losing weight and withdrawing from friends and neighbors. She could not dispose of her husband's clothing or a large collection of tools he kept in a metal shed behind their home. She had always taken great pride in her yard. Now it was a shambles.

As the anniversary date of her husband's death approached, we were worried. People in the grief support group worked out a plan to have two widows visit her on the morning of the anniversary date. I was to see her in the afternoon. Someone else would invite her to dinner that evening.

When the day arrived, the two women went to see Lucy. They found her out in the yard busily putting in new plants. The tools were gone, sold to a neighbor. The shed was now her garden-supply area. She wasn't home when I went to call because she had gone to a bridge club with a neighbor. At dinner that evening, she told her hosts that she had completed her responsibility to mourn and now it was time to get on with her life. She has remained a happy and well person who is continuing to find new ways to enjoy life.

Mark the anniversary of your loss in some way. You can decide to take charge of this day. I suggest:

❖ *If you work, take the day off. You may want to treat yourself to a night luxuriating at a bed and breakfast while someone else cooks your meals.*

❖ *Make a conscious effort to recall your loved one. Go back in your journal and read your entries for the year. Read your letter of good-bye.*

❖ *Make phone calls or write notes of thanks to everyone you can think of who was helpful to you throughout the year.*

❖ *Arrange a dinner date with a good friend who knows all about your loss.*

❖ *Using the exercise for goal setting on page 168, make new plans for the next year.*

❖ *If you are living in a new city or state, visit your old home area or call someone you know there.*

❖ *Begin studying your new area. Learn something of*
   its history.

Whatever your loss, make the anniversary a specific
time you look forward to with at least as much hope as
you look back in sorrow. As you begin the second year
after your loss, it is time to begin focusing your attention
more on where you are going than where you have been.

The Eighteenth Month

This is the point in time when you find out your grief isn't
finished. By the time you are a year and a half away from
your loss, you are sure the rough places are behind you.
You are having more good days than bad ones. You may
have even learned to laugh again. All of a sudden, it may
seem as though you are back at the beginning of grief
again. Sadness returns. Thoughts of the deceased person
dominate your attention. Nights that were finally tolerable
get long and tough again. If you are divorced you may have
gone through 18 months of sheer euphoria at gaining your
freedom only to have the bottom suddenly drop out from
under your emotions.

What you need to learn at this point is that you are
responding in a very normal way to a major loss. Very often
this is when people turn to a grief support group for the
first time. Dorothy heard about our group from a friend.
She walked in one day to say, "I thought I had this thing
licked. I never did go through some of the things people
told me to expect after my husband's death. Everything
was going along fine until early this month. Now I feel like
I'm headed backward." When I inquired how long ago
Dorothy's husband had died she said it had been 18
months.

Dr. Glen Davidson's study of bereaved people demonstrated the frequency of this return to a more intense level
of grieving. The graph shows the sudden return of this

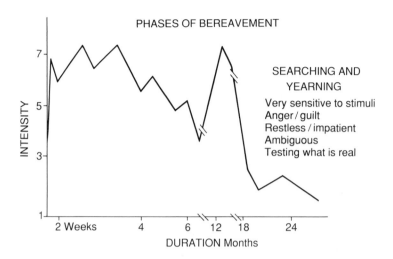

PHASES OF BEREAVEMENT

SEARCHING AND
YEARNING

Very sensitive to stimuli
Anger / guilt
Restless / impatient
Ambiguous
Testing what is real

Intensity of the characteristics of mourning in the first months after the death of a loved one. Reprinted by permission from *Understanding Mourning* by Glen W. Davidson ©1984 Augsburg Publishing House.

intensity between the twelfth and eighteenth months after the death of a loved one.

The most important things to know about this bump in the road to recovery are:

❖ *It is a sign of progress, not regression.*

❖ *It doesn't last long.*

❖ *The best way to handle it is to do the things you would do if the loss were a recent one.*

Beyond the Second Year

Once you have passed the second anniversary of your loss, your primary focus will be on adapting to the new life you are finding. Sometimes, the greatest challenge is to admit you are ready to move on.

❖ *You may struggle with a sense of being disloyal to a deceased spouse.*

❖ *If one of your parents has died and the surviving
   one begins to date another person or remarries,
   you may have a problem with anger.*

❖ *Parents who lose a child to death often choose this
   time to begin planning for the birth of another
   child.*

❖ *For most divorcing people, the beginning of the
   third year is when the old marriage is put behind.
   You may begin to waver in your resolve never to
   marry again.*

You will find that the pain of your grief is not as intense
anymore. Special dates and occasions may still cause you to
become emotional, but in general you will be more able to
begin finding what life has in store for you now.

This a time to begin making longer-range plans for yourself. It may be the occasion for a new wardrobe or hairstyle.
It is a good time to give your loss meaning by using the things
you have learned to help others who are grieving.

The End of Grief

It is a terrible lie that says the end of your grief is
emptiness and despair. Each of these special points in
time are mileposts along the way to recovery.

You will not always feel as you do in the beginning,
middle or end of grief. If you will enter into it with
understanding of what to expect of yourself, you will
find joyful surprises along with the disappointments.

Grief is not something you should avoid. It is more
difficult and painful than anything else you will face in
life. It takes a long time to get through it. But it can also
be an unparalleled occasion for discovery of your own
strength of character.

The person who drew me into my involvement with
grief and loss is Frieda. When her husband died after a

lengthy battle with cancer, I expected Frieda to fall apart. George had been one of those big, super-macho men who could do anything. He was a strong personality who dominated his family. Frieda seemed to lean on him for her support and I wondered if she would survive George's death.

However, from the beginning, I saw a new Frieda emerge. She became the guiding force in the development of our first grief support group. She helped one newly bereaved person after another see the need to gather together so they could help each other. She encouraged me to risk leading the group. Her open sharing of what she was experiencing week by week taught me my first lesson in understanding the process of healthy grief.

A little more than a year after George's death Frieda announced to the group that she had remodeled her bedroom. Gone was the massive dark furniture that was characteristic of George. In its place she had a new bed with pink frilly covers, feminine decorations and new wallpaper.

Frieda's grief was deep and her loss extremely hard for her to handle. But she gave it all she had. In so doing she found a strength of character that surprised her more than anyone else. Today she is continuing to build a meaningful life for herself.

Frieda found what you can find. Grief is as much about finding as it is about losing. It is not a social disease, but a process of recovering your balance after life has dealt you a major blow.

Enduring the stresses and challenges of grief recovery calls for a discipline that can add a valuable dimension to your life. You can emerge from it considerably stronger and more compassionate than you were before.

Making these discoveries gives direction and purpose to your grief and empowers you to live your new life with hope and joy.

14

Choosing to
Live Again

Taking charge of your own grief

AS THE WEEKS GO BY after a major loss, some normal routines will return to your life.

If you are employed, the need for income will take you back to work. If you are the parent of young children, you will find their lives go on and so do their demands for attention. Pets still have to be looked after and fed. Bills must be paid. Household tasks and yard work have not taken a vacation while you were in shock.

Granted, nothing is exactly the same as it was before you lost a loved one to death or divorce, or moved to a strange new town or faced some other major loss. The tasks may be the same, but you are not!

The work that was all but automatic for you may now

seem all but impossible. The normal cries of your children may grate on your nerves.

Routine household chores have now become exercises in drudgery.

Your energy level will be very low. You may want excessive amounts of sleep, or lie staring at the ceiling night after night.

As you move beyond the first few weeks, the permanence of your loss comes home, and with that realization comes the pain. The usual demands on your life call again for your attention. But now, the pain feels like trying to go through a normal day with the worst toothache you've ever had in your life.

Choosing to Live Again

There is one decision confronting you that dominates all others at this point in time: *You must choose to live again.*

Choosing to live again means taking charge of your grief. For the first week or two, much of your life was out of control. Chances are your grief owned you. Now it is time for you to own your grief and to direct the pathway of your recovery.

You have been knocked off-balance—flattened like a pancake is probably a better description. And now it's time to get up again, recover your sense of balance and get on with your life.

Giving Yourself Permission to Grieve

This exercise takes grief out of the category of things that shouldn't happen and makes it a symbol of your capacity to love.

If you have had a major loss recently, grief doesn't seem like something that requires permission. Grief for you is a "dirty word." It describes something horrible. It's nothing to be proud of and you wish it would just go away as quickly as possible.

I want you to give yourself permission to experience another kind of grief.

You will need an 8-1/2" x 11" tablet of lined paper.

Follow these steps in exactly the sequence listed:

1. Describe the loss that has brought you grief. How long ago did it happen?

2. Write as much as you want to about the importance of your relationship with that person, place or condition that is lost.

3. Describe the pain and sadness you feel because of the loss. The list of feeling words in Appendix A may help you describe your feelings more clearly.

4. What is the impact of this loss on your total life? What else have you lost because of this loss?

5. Read your responses to numbers 2, 3 and 4 aloud.

6. What do your responses tell you about your affection for the person, place or condition that was lost?

7. Considering the love you have for whoever or whatever was lost, and the impact of that loss on your total life, would any other response from you except grief be appropriate?

8. Write the following on a clean sheet of paper: "The sadness I feel is a badge of honor. I wear the brokenness of my life at this moment with pride. These expressions of my grief testify to the importance of _____ and the depth of my love for (him/her/place/condition). I am willing to feel the full impact of my grief as a final act of tribute and love. I will make my way through this experience and will not run from it."

Sign your name to the statement.

9. Make four copies. Keep the original for yourself and post it in a conspicuous place.

Send the copies to four other persons, at least two of whom are not family members. You may want to include your clergy.

What you will have done with this exercise is establish a purpose for your sadness and take charge of directing your own recovery.

Facing a Loss from the Past

If you described an event from the past by several years, you will not require the same amount of time to work through it. However, the grief you are experiencing is no less real.

June was over 50 years old when she first realized she had been sexually molested as a young child. For all those years the trauma of that terrible event had lain in the recesses of her emotions, too painful to be allowed into consciousness. When the awareness finally came, a deep sadness and grief accompanied it.

Over the course of several months she dug into her painful feelings about her loss. She called it a *loss of innocence*. Her basic trust of life had been damaged. She had gone through 31 years of marriage, never understanding why she could not fully enjoy intimacy. It seemed to her as if she had been robbed of many of life's joys.

There was no way to recover those lost years or the joy they might have had. She was filled with anger, hurt and frustration.

Using a method like the exercise you have just completed, June was able to work through the grief and take charge of her response to a deep wound in her life.

Today she has fully recovered her balance in relation to that event. She openly shares her experience to help other women deal with this very painful loss.

As her husband, I am very proud of her.

Giving yourself permission to grieve is a great gift. It is an important step in recovering from a present or past loss and an important key to a full life after loss.

Keeping a Journal of Your Journey through Grief

Once you have given yourself permission to grieve, the next important thing for you to do is keep a daily journal of your journey through grief. Use a stenographer's notebook or a diary. Indicate the date and time of the entry at the top of each page. Include this information for each day:

❖ *A significant event that happened*

❖ *The person who was most important to me today*

❖ *Changes I observe happening to me*

❖ *My plans for tomorrow*

❖ *Notes to myself*

Make your entries in the evening after dinner and at least an hour before you go to bed.

The importance of a daily journal will only become evident to you some months, maybe as long as a year, down the road. The changes that mark your progress through grief come slowly. You may think you are making no progress at all and become more discouraged. At times like these, reading back through your journal will help you remember where you have been and how far you have really come.

The journal helps you stay in charge of your grief experience.

❖ *Writing down the events of each day gives these events significance.*

❖ *Thinking about people who are important to you keeps you from further loneliness.*

❖ *Always noting your plans for the next day encourages a positive direction.*

I suggest you make your journal entries in the evening

because when you are struggling with grief, the evenings are almost always the most difficult time of the day. By intentionally focusing on your grief at this time, you take charge of your experience. I call it *de-spooking the evenings.* It works.

When you've finished writing in your journal, you may want to read or do some other activity that is relaxing.

It is a good idea to drink only herb teas, decaffeinated coffee or plain water while you work with your journal. You are doing this in the evening and caffeinated or high-sugar beverages may interfere with restful sleep later.

If you have problems relaxing, the next exercises can be helpful. I like them because they are simple and effective.

An Exercise to Relax Tension

This exercise is known as the *8-8-8 Breather.*

Sit in a comfortable chair with your feet on the floor and your hands laid loosely on your thighs, palms down. Close your eyes. Do the following:

1. Gently blow out all the air in your lungs.
2. *Slowly* inhale while counting to eight. Allow your abdomen to expand while you are breathing in. Count: one-and-two-and-three-and...up to eight.
3. Hold your breath to the same count of eight.
4. *Slowly* exhale while counting to eight in the same manner. Relax your abdomen as you breathe out.
5. Breathe normally for about one minute.
6. Repeat this sequence several times until you feel your tension subsiding.

A Variation on Counting Sheep

This relaxation exercise can be done anytime, but is particularly helpful when you can't get to sleep.

Lie down in bed on your back with legs straight and hands by your sides.

Do the 8-8-8 Breather exercise several times.

Close your eyes and look as far up inside your eyelids as you can.

Begin counting silently simultaneously from 1 to 100, and from 100 to 1. It is done like this: 100-1, 99-2, 98-3, 97-4, 96-5.... Keep your eyes looking up inside your eyelids.

As you continue to count, you will find your eyes becoming tired. Allow them to relax to a comfortable position.

At some point you will begin to have difficulty keeping track of the sequence of numbers. This is a sign your mind is beginning to relax and prepare for sleep. Don't try to force the sequence to continue.

When this happens, picture a descending stairway in front of you. It is 20 steps in length and is of any design you wish. There is a landing halfway down.

Picture yourself slowly descending the stairs one step at a time. Count them as you go. One-two-three-four...when you reach ten, pause on the landing. Then, slowly descend the rest of the way.

You may not reach the bottom before falling asleep. *Don't fight it!*

If you do get all the way down, you will feel very relaxed and at ease. Picture a room that is your own private retreat. No one else ever shares this space with you. It is decorated and arranged exactly as you want it to be. It is warm and comfortable. In this place you are free from all pressures and concerns. Allow yourself to be in this room for as long as you want.

Even if you do not fall asleep, you will be resting. I have found 20 minutes of this kind of relaxation to be as refreshing as two or three hours of normal sleep.

As a variation during the day, you can sit in a comfortable chair, fix your eyes on some small object or mark on a wall, and begin counting until your eyes grow heavy. Then allow them to close and begin descending the staircase. When you reach your room at the bottom, remain there as long as you wish. When you are ready to end the relaxation period, count your way back up the stairs. Your eyes will open near the top and you will feel quite refreshed and alert.

When You Just Can't Sleep

Sometimes, in spite of all your best efforts, you will wake up in the middle of the night and not be able to go back to sleep. It seems to take only a night or two of interrupted sleep to get the cycle started, but it can take months to get back to normal. This exercise will help you re-program your sleeping habits within a week or two.

First create a daily calendar of the things you are going to do. Divide each 24-hour period into four parts: mornings (after your usual waking time), afternoons, evenings (up to your normal bedtime) and nighttime (normal sleeping hours). Plan your time as follows:

Morning: List what you will do from the time you get up until you have lunch. Schedule your lunch at a specific hour and have it whether you feel like eating or not.

Afternoon: List what you will do after lunch until time for dinner. Also schedule that meal at a specific hour and eat it.

Evening: List the hours of the evening from dinner time until bedtime. Example: if you eat at 6:00 p.m. and normally go to bed at 10:00 p.m. your schedule would be:

6:00 p.m. Dinner
7:00 p.m.
8:00 p.m.
9:00 p.m.
10:00 p.m. Bedtime

Now fill in what you will do each hour of the evening. Try to follow through with each hour's plan.

Nighttime: List the time that you are waking most

frequently during the night. Then list each half hour from that time until your normal waking time. For instance, if you normally get up at 6:00 a.m., but now are waking each night at 2:00 a.m., your list would look like this:

2:00 a.m.
2:30 a.m.
3:00 a.m.
3:30 a.m.
4:00 a.m.
4:30 a.m.
5:00 a.m.
5:30 a.m.
6:00 a.m.

Each evening write down what you will do in 30-minute increments from the time you wake up until your normal rising time. *This is crucial:* Give yourself tasks to do that are unpleasant. Clean cupboards or toilets, mop floors, balance your checkbook—anything that you do not like to do! There should be no snacking and no lying in bed staring at the ceiling.

If you go back to bed, use one of the relaxing techniques to put yourself to sleep again. Most people find that after a few nights of this regimen they are sleeping until their normal rising time without further problems.

Learning to relax is an important skill for you to master as you work your way through grief and learn to live again. So is changing your attitude about crying.

A Programmed Cry

This exercise is specifically designed to help you get rid of your fears, fantasies and reservations about crying. You will probably use it more than once in the first weeks and months after a major loss. It demonstrates clearly that your emotions do not have to be kept under a tight rein, even in the face of the worst of losses.

Preparation

You will be okay. However, to alleviate any unnecessary anxiety, choose someone to be your caretaker. This person should know what you are doing and be familiar with the circumstances of your grief. You will have your caretaker's telephone number by your phone in case you need assistance.

Choose a room in your home that has sentimental importance for you. Supplies should include some large pillows, a full box of tissues, a radio and photographs of the one who is gone. Do the exercise in the evening.

How to cry

Turn the lights low. Turn on soft music. Select a station that plays sentimental music with few interruptions, or use records or tapes. Turn the volume as loud as is comfortable.

Feel the impact of the mood you have created. Allow it to touch your sadness. Think about the person who has died or the dreams for a happy marriage that are gone. Or look at photographs of the people and places you left when you moved to a new city.

Remember the most intimate times. Think about your loss. Turn your feelings loose. Say what you are feeling aloud.

Put two chairs back to back. Sit in one and imagine the person or people you have lost in the other. Talk directly to the one you have lost. Say what you are feeling aloud.

As an alternative, you may want to picture God sitting in the chair. Tell God your feelings about your loss without restraint.

Hold a pillow in your arms and cry into it. Rock back and forth. Yell if you want to. Call out your loss. Feel it completely. Let your feelings go for as long as they want to come out.

Know that you are being healed by the release of all the pain and sadness. Don't try to hide your anger.

When you begin to feel better, allow that new feeling to emerge. Concentrate your attention on the positive thoughts that you are having. Say those positive thoughts aloud.

When you are ready, turn up the lights. Turn the music low. Change its mood to something happy and bright. Put away all the symbols of your weeping—the tissues, pillow, chairs.

Do breathing exercises; stretch your muscles; do some simple calisthenics or run in place.

Drink a large glass or two of water. Make some herbal tea or have fruit or vegetable juice. Snack on fresh fruits or vegetables, crackers, pretzels or popcorn.

Take a warm bath or shower. Read a humorous book. Go to sleep.

As soon as possible tell your caretaker about the experience. Tell your counselor or grief support group.

Record your experience in your journal.

You will find that most of your hesitancy and discomfort with tears are gone. You will be able to experience your feelings more easily and with less anxiety.

Many people have found this exercise to be like turning on the lights in a dark room. All the mystery and myth associated with the act of crying disappears. Instead of tears being a problem for you in working through your grief, they become a resource for healing. Once you are more comfortable with crying, you are ready to confront your grief itself in a more direct way.

Communicating with Your Grief

This exercise does to grief what the last one did to crying. It dispels the notion that grief is a six-headed monster of some kind who will get you if you mention his name. The task here is to communicate with your grief as though it has a personality of its own. You will talk to your grief and you will listen to your grief.

If your loved one has died, this is an especially helpful exercise about three months after the death.

You are going to write two letters. I suggest using whatever stationery you normally use for writing to friends or family. See pages 90-91 for an example.

The first letter is from you to your grief. Use the following form:

Date:_____ Time:_____

To Grief,

Sincerely,
(your name)

Before you write, ask yourself, "If I could tell my grief what I am thinking and feeling, what would I say? What do I want my grief to know about its impact on my life?"

Be as frank as you can. Write the letter and sign it.

As close to 24 hours later, but no less than that, write the second letter. This one will be from your grief to you.

Use the same format as the first letter, except address it to yourself and sign it, "Sincerely, Grief."

Before writing, ask yourself: What do I think my grief is telling me? What does it want from me?

Then, as frankly as possible, write to yourself on behalf of your grief.

Put the letters aside for a day or two, then read them both aloud to yourself.

What do the letters reveal about your attitude toward the experience of grief? What new thing can you learn about yourself from the letters?

Find someone with whom you can share the letters and talk about your discoveries. If you are in a support group, this is an excellent activity to share with each other.

I suggest you keep your letters with your journal.

About two years later write the same letters again without referring to the originals, then compare your responses. You will be amazed that the same person wrote both sets of letters! You may find the second set sounding as if they were written by an adventurer more than a griever.

If communicating with your grief is a problem, so is communicating with your friends, family and co-workers. There aren't many people around who will be comfortable with your grief. Very soon after any major loss, including death and divorce, folks will want you to at least act as if you are choosing to live again. They will want you to do this long before you are ready for it.

Anthropologist Margaret Mead said, "When a person is born we celebrate; when they marry we are jubilant; but, when they die we act as if nothing has happened." Why?, because birth and marriage are occasions when loss is dominated by joyful gain. We know what to say and how to react in those occasions. But we see death as the great Canceled Stamp to every aspect of human joy. We don't know what to say to a bereaved person. We are terribly uncomfortable in the presence of someone else's grief.

That's good to remember when it's our turn to grieve. When people stay away at the time we need them most it's not that they don't love us. They just don't know what to say or do. They feel helpless.

This exercise is designed to help you communicate with those whose support you need the most. This includes family members, friends, clergy and doctors.

Things to Remember about Non-grievers

Type or write the following sentences on a card or piece of paper and carry it with you for the first nine months of your grief experience.

1. I will not expect others to be better at handling my grief than I would have been at handling theirs before my loss.

2. People cannot be something other than who they are.

3. Most people want to help me. They mean well even when they do dumb and hurtful things.

4. Others, including professional people, will not know what is helpful to me unless I tell them.

5. I will be as patient with others as I need them to be with me.

Carry this information with you so it is readily available. You will want to read it for comfort several times each day as other people do incredibly uncaring things. For example, if your spouse has died it won't be long before somebody:

❖ *Asks you how you are doing and you will know the only acceptable answer is "fine."*

❖ *Acts as if your deceased husband or wife never had a name. This will happen at a time when you want everyone to know that he or she was a special person who will always be a part of your life.*

❖ *Finds a way to avoid talking to you.*

❖ *Questions some decision you made about the funeral, burial or events preceding the person's death.*

If you understand that other people's poor reactions are not your fault, it will remove one more burden from the load you are already carrying.

Things to Tell Non-grievers

Have the following statements typed or printed on good-quality, colored paper. I suggest having a quick-print store do it for you. Almost every town has one and they have all the supplies you need.

My Dear (Family, Friends, Pastor, Employer...)

I have experienced a loss that is devastating to me. It will take time, perhaps years, for me to work through the grief I am having because of this loss.

I will cry more than usual for some time. My tears are not a sign of weakness or a lack of hope or faith. They are the symbols of the depth of my loss and the sign that I am recovering.

I may become angry without there seeming to be a reason for it. My emotions are all heightened by the stress of grief. Please be forgiving if I seem irrational at times.

I need your understanding and your presence more than anything else. If you don't know what to say, just touch me or give me a hug to let me know you care. Please don't wait for me to call you. I am often too tired to even think of reaching out for the help I need.

Don't allow me to withdraw from you. I need you more than ever during the next year.

Pray for me only if your prayer is not an order for me to make you feel better. My faith is not an excuse from the process of grief.

If you, by chance, have had an experience of loss that seems anything like mine, please share it with me. You will not make me feel worse.

This loss is the worst thing that could happen to me. But, I will get through it and I will live again. I will not always feel as I do now. I will laugh again.

Thank you for caring about me. Your concern is a gift I will always treasure.

Sincerely, (your name)

Alter this sample letter in whatever way suits your circumstances. Give a copy to those whose support you need most. By putting thoughts such as these in writing you will avoid much misunderstanding. People will know more of what to expect of you and from you.

You are also affirming in a very strong way that you intend to be in charge of your grief experience and to grow through it.

Getting on with Life

Making the decision to live again after a major loss is not easy. It requires putting your willpower and thought power ahead of some very powerful emotions.

You cannot wait until you feel better and then decide to live again. You must make the decision because you know it's right, and then wait for your feelings to catch up. They will.

The next chapter contains more exercises to help you carry out your decision and establish a high-quality new life after your loss.

15

Opening New Doors

Decisions that make a difference

DECISION MAKING IS ONE of the most difficult challenges you will face as you work at recovering your balance after a major loss.

In the first few days, as you face endless demands, you operate like a robot as you go through the motions of decision making.

Later the numbness and shock wears off and you experience excruciating pain. Making *any* decision takes maximum effort. At first, it is all the paperwork that follows a death or divorce; the tasks of locating necessary services in a new town or adjusting to life without one of your limbs.

Later, decision making has a new dimension. The

pressure now is not so much what you *have* to do as what you *want* to do. It is time to move on. You know now that you will survive your loss.

The pain is still there and at times it hurts as much as ever. But at least now you are used to it. It may seem as if the terrible emptiness and sadness in the pit of your stomach and the ache in your heart have always been there. You are sure these things will be a part of you for a long time.

Six months after her husband died, Cindy came to see me in a new state of shock. A man in her office had asked her for a date! The mere fact that she had a decision to make stunned her. She was single. She didn't think of herself that way. Like most widows, she differed from divorced singles in that she saw herself as a married person whose husband was dead. Her divorced friends saw themselves as single and available to the right person.

For Cindy the difficulty in saying "yes" or "no" to a date was that either answer acknowledged she now had decisions to make and a life to live without Hal.

I think that's also the reason so many divorced persons are crushed by the news of their ex-spouse's remarriage. It simply drives home the fact that the past is really gone. There is no recovering it, and life must now go on.

There comes a time in recovering from the grief of any major loss when you will seem to be standing in a large, cold room with no windows, but many, many doors. You will know that you must leave this room sometime. It is not a pleasant place, but nevertheless, choosing a door isn't easy.

The room is filled with the memories and images of your past and the terrible loss you have experienced. You aren't sure that what waits beyond any of the doors is better. You hope so, but you can't see how life can ever be warm and cozy again.

To leave the room is to leave your past. You can take

your memories with you, but that's all.

Any choice you make will take you on to a new and different life that you have never lived before.

It's time to choose.

Earl Grollman says in his book, *Time Remembered:*

> *"It's a risk to attempt new beginnings...Yet the greater risk is for you to risk nothing. For there will be no further possibilities of learning and changing, of traveling upon the journey of life...You were strong to hold on. You will be stronger to go forward to new beginnings."* [1]

An Exercise in Setting Goals

In your journal or in a separate tablet, put the date at the top of a page and answer these questions.

1. What tasks do I need to complete in the next seven days? If I didn't have to do these things, what would I *like* to do in the next seven days?

2. What barriers are there to keep me from doing the things I most want to do?

3. What resources do I have to overcome these barriers?

4. Whose help do I need to do the things I want to do?

5. What things would I like to do in the next 90 days?

6. What spiritual resources do I need to find or recover to help me go on with my life?

7. What would my life look like one year from today if I could have my way?

Choose one goal each from your seven-day, 90-day and one-year lists. Write each of these goals and indicate how you will know when you have reached each of them:

7 days

90 days

1 year

Select one spiritual resource you would like to find or recover. Make an appointment to discuss this goal with your minister, priest or rabbi. If you do not belong to a religious community, ask a friend for a referral.

Make a diary notation on your calendar to check on your seven-day goal a week from this date.

Begin working on each of the goals you selected no later than the day after the date on the top of your questionnaire.

Keep a record in your journal of your progress on each of the goals you selected. If you accomplish one, choose another from the same category. If it becomes obvious that a goal is unrealistic, choose an alternate. If a new goal surfaces, go for it.

Share your goals and the dates for completion with a friend who will hold you accountable.

At the end of the first week, set a new goal for the next seven days. Continue this procedure for at least the first year.

By setting short-, medium- and long-range goals for yourself, you are beginning to open the doors to your future. Whether or not you reach all of the goals doesn't matter. The most important thing is that you are beginning to make new choices for your life after loss.

The next step is a painful one. I want you to know that up front before you begin the exercise. It is also a very important one to your continued recovery.

Writing a Letter of Good-bye

Saying good-bye is never easy. When your guests go home or you leave favorite relatives after a visit, the time of parting has an element of sadness to it.

To say good-bye to a deceased loved one, the end of a marriage or the places and people you called home hurts beyond words.

However, before you can open new doors for your life, you have to close the ones that are now in the past. It doesn't mean forgetting the person or memories any more than you forget your friends when they go home after dinner.

To say good-bye acknowledges you will not share life with a person, place, stage of life or part of your body anymore.

It is an act of lovingly releasing a part of your life that will always remain important to you in memory, but which you must now live without.

It is important to say good-bye as you part temporarily from folks you care about, and it's more important to say good-bye to those you will not see again in this life. It is just as important to bid good-bye to lost places and dreams.

Because you can't say good-bye to the one who has died or the marriage that has ended, the next alternative is to write a letter. If you are like most people, it will be the most difficult letter you have ever written. It will help if you understand it is also one of the most important letters you will ever write.

To begin, think about whomever or whatever was lost to you that is the source of your grief. Go back to your journal and look at the things you wrote in the exercise titled, *Giving Yourself Permission to Grieve.*

Use your favorite stationery for this letter. If you don't have a supply, buy some as though you were writing to someone very important. Use a good pen. This letter deserves the best you've got. No pencils or notebook paper, please.

Address your letter as follows: If it is to a deceased person, use the salutation you used in life with this person. If it is to a marriage that is now over, address the focus of your loss as if it were a person. That may or may not be your ex-spouse. If it is to a place, address it as if it were a person. (June and I wrote to "Our Dear Home...") If it is a broken dream, a business failure or a stage of life, address it in a personal way.

After addressing your letter, acknowledge immediately that it is a letter of good-bye. Then proceed to tell the person or personalized event anything you would like to have said, but didn't.

Express thanks for specific things you will remember.

If you are writing to a deceased loved one, give your permission for that person to be dead.

Share your hopes and vision for the life you will live after your loss.

Sign the letter in whatever way is appropriate for you.

Wait about 24 hours and then read your letter aloud to yourself. Read it aloud several times each day for several days. When you can read it all the way through, even with tears, read it aloud to a friend, counselor or clergy.

Keep the letter with your journal and other written exercises as a historic moment along your journey to recovery.

Ken wrote the following as part of his letter after the death of his wife:

My darling Mae,

You and I always had our Lord with us. If it weren't so, I don't know what I would do now. That is what sustained us through your illness and now my faith and trust in my beloved Lord is what sustains me.

The great void your death has left in my life is still a gaping hole. How can a "we" become an "I"? How can an "us" become a "me"? How can an "our" become a "mine"?

Because of God, I believe there will always be a "we" and an "us" and an "our" in my heart. By faith I can release you to the love and care of our Lord until we will meet again in his Kingdom.

Ken

This letter helped Ken release his attachment to Mae and move on to a new life for himself that in time included another wife.

Martha's loss was the marriage she thought would last forever. After 11 years, it was over. She and Brad had shared a common dream for the first few years. As they struggled through a career change for him, she worked to help support them, sacrificing her own vocational goals.

She imagined that once he was established in his new career, it would be her turn to return to school. When the day came that Brad had a good job with a promising future in front of them, Martha quit her job and enrolled in night school. Brad was furious. He wanted her to work until their debt for his education was paid off. Their fights over money spread to the subject of having children. He was ready. She wasn't.

Outwardly, they looked like an ideal couple. In private, the words grew ever more harsh and the times of happiness became rare. It all ended when Martha came home unexpectedly in the middle of the day to find Brad in bed with another woman.

After the divorce became final, I suggested Martha write a letter of good-bye to Brad and their marriage. At first, I think she was sure I had lost my mind. In time, Martha did write the letter. Here is an excerpt:

Bradley,

As I write this letter to say good-bye to you, I refuse to add the word, "Dear." I don't think I will ever forgive you for what you did to me, although I'm told this anger I feel will be more costly to me than to you. It's hard for me to remember that the first six years of our marriage were so good. I think it's knowing that once I loved you so much (and I think you loved me too) that hurts the most.

It feels as if something inside of me has been

murdered. I feel so sad and so angry, all at the same time. My only hope is that one day I will be able to remember the good times without having my thoughts dominated by the ugliness of the last two years.

I am trying to put my life together again. I have started going to church again and that gives me some peace, at least for a little while. I am going to night school and doing well and that helps me to feel better about myself.

I don't miss you and all the hassles, but I do hate being alone so much. I can't even stand the thought of getting involved with another man. He'd probably turn out to be like you. Maybe someday. First, I will get to know me and what I want much better than I do now.

I believe there is a good life for me in the future because I believe I am a good person.

Brad, this is hard for me to say, but thanks for the early years. Our picnic breakfasts in the park and laughter we shared about our first little apartment are memories I want to keep.

Good-bye. I hope you will remember some good things about being with me too.

Martha

By reading her letter aloud several times, Martha was able to identify her anger and begin the process of releasing it. Over the next several months she was able to see more of her own failure in the marriage. In time she received a college degree and she is now doing well in her career. When I last saw her, Martha was still single.

Using the Resources of Religion

Regardless of whether or not you have been an actively religious person, the resources of religion are important for you.

Grief is not first of all an intellectual experience. Philosophical religious concepts aren't going to help you. This is no time for theological debates about the "right" kind of religion.

I urge you to find the clergyperson and church or synagogue in your area that has the best program for grief support. Whatever the religious orientation of the group, it will help you.

The resources that religion offers best are hope, comfort and a sense of some greater meaning to life. You will benefit from all of these as you begin to open new doors to your life.

Starting a Grief Support Group

The best support system while working through your grief is a group of other people who have also experienced loss. One of the new doors you can choose to open is organizing and starting such a group. It may sound difficult, but I assure you it isn't.

A grief support group doesn't require a highly trained, professional leader to be effective. It is an added bonus if one is available, especially as the group gets started. You may be able to find a counselor who will act as a referral resource if someone in the group shows signs of distorted grief.

Loss and grief are such common experiences that announcing almost anywhere that you are forming a support group will produce the people you need. A group doesn't have to be larger than three or four, and should not exceed eight or 10 without a trained leader.

The exercises I have given you in this book are useful

as group activities. All of them have been tested over a minimum of five years in groups I have led.

Your church or synagogue can be an excellent source of people for the group. Your pastor, priest or rabbi may provide a meeting place and perhaps help with the leadership.

A grief support group should plan to meet for a minimum of 12 sessions on a weekly basis for 1 to 1-1/2 hours per session. I personally like the ongoing model where people can come for as long as they wish. This model also provides a ready-made referral place for newly bereaved persons.

When someone's grief becomes distorted, the group provides a loving atmosphere in which seeking professional counseling can be urged.

How long should you have a support group? As long as you feel the need and until you have opened all the doors to new life that you want to open.

Remember, the entire first year after a major loss is dominated by experiences of "the first time without." For at least that year you need all the support you can get.

A support group also allows you to make your own loss have meaning by using your experience to help others. That's no little thing!

Appendix C contains a more detailed description of how to call a group together and what to do during the first few sessions.

Making Your Loss Become a Creative Hurt

When you get involved with the grief of other people you should know one thing: Sharing in the grief of others is like playing in the mud. You can't do it without getting some on you!

There will be times when you are sure you have all the load you can carry with your own grief. You won't see how you could handle that of anyone else.

However, there is a marvelous mystery about grief. The more you share in the grief of others, the more in charge of your own grief you will be. It won't be any less painful. But it will seem considerably more manageable.

When you share your struggles and discoveries with others and listen to their stories, you will find your pain becoming a creative hurt. It will have purpose, meaning, and a dignity that you didn't sense before.

The people I know who have most fully recovered their balance after a major loss are those who gave the most of themselves to others.

Jeanne lost her husband of 49 years after a brief illness. She was past 70 at the time. They had no children. Shortly after Alan's death, Jeanne began pouring her life into the needs of others. She befriended a young mother whose husband committed suicide, cared for a sister until her death at age 93, and became the source of hope for another widow who was struggling with a drinking problem. Now, past age 85, she volunteers at a community food bank and serves on the council for a preschool.

Mary, widowed many years younger than Jeanne, has become a volunteer in the surgery waiting room of the hospital where her husband died. Dorothy, whose husband has been a victim of Alzheimer's disease for several years, fills the loneliness of her life by volunteering at a local school. She works as a teacher's aid with first graders who dearly love her attention.

Al poured himself into volunteer work at his church after his wife's death to cancer. He sings in the choir, helps in the office and chairs the personnel committee.

The opportunities and the needs are endless. It's another step on the path to recovery that's often difficult to take, but the rewards are plentiful. I can't diagram an exercise to tell you how to turn the pain of your grief into a creative hurt. I can only tell you that the opportunities are there if you will open the doors before you.

Another door that is always before you sometime after a major loss is the need to give forgiveness to someone. Your failure to open this door can block your ability to release the past and move fully into a new life.

An Exercise in Forgiveness

Two almost surefire spin-offs of grief are anger and broken relationships. It is as true in the case of a death as it is with a divorce. It is a factor in relocation and other major losses.

I believe you can make this assumption and never be wrong: *If you have experienced grief, there is someone you need to forgive.*

It's possible, of course, that there is someone who needs to forgive *you*. But that is *their* task. Your need to forgive is your task.

Begin with this survey, using a clean piece of paper.

At the top, write the name of a person with whom you have had conflict or from whom you have felt alienated since your loss.

What is your relationship with this person? Is he or she a family member or friend? How long have you known this person?

Do you blame this person in any way for your loss? If so, how?

Are you angry, resentful or hateful toward this person? If so, why?

What is happening to you because of the break in your relationship with this person?

Can you forgive this person and express your forgiveness? If you are able to forgive, write down a date on which you will offer your forgiveness. Also note if you will express it in person, on the telephone or by letter.

Granting forgiveness is never easy and can be very difficult under the stress of grief. You may think you would be disloyal to the one who has died or to your own

principles if there has been a divorce. You may feel vulnerable or fear looking weak.

If your anger is still unresolved and you are unable to
think of forgiving, continue this exercise, using another
piece of paper.

How is your self-esteem being affected by your anger?
In what ways are you being robbed of energy? Is your
sleep being affected?

Write down the name of a trusted friend, counselor or
clergy. Share this survey and your struggle to forgive with
this person.

Determine why you are not able to forgive. Find the
deeper reasons for your hurt and anger.

Write a letter of forgiveness to the person whether or
not you feel forgiving. Write as if you wanted to forgive.
Place the letter in an envelope and put it in your journal.
Each day as you make your entry, read the letter aloud to
yourself. Make changes in the letter as your feelings
change. Stay with it until you can begin to feel forgiving.

*Do not mail the letter or act on it until you are sure
you are fully ready to forgive.* I suggest choosing an
occasion that has special meaning to act on your forgiveness.

Reaching out with forgiveness will bring more healing
to you than to the one you forgive.

The Importance of Touch

During those first few days after your loss, when shock and
numbness have shut down your emotional system, nothing else will communicate caring to you quite as much as
the touch of another person.

Over the course of the ensuing months, you will ap-
preciate those people who don't try to find the right words
to say, but are just there with a touch on the arm or a timely
hug.

The touch of another human being counts more when

you have experienced a major loss than any other time in your life.

I learned this while on call to a local hospital. My staff and I were providing supplemental pastoral services to the one full-time Protestant chaplain. The first emergency call I received was to the infant intensive-care unit.

A baby had been born prematurely and wasn't making it. When I arrived, the newborn infant was hooked to special machines that did his breathing and monitored his every function. After some time it was clear that he simply was not developed enough to survive.

The time had come to make the decision to unhook the life support. I held hands with the parents as the wires and tubes were removed. We took the baby to the mother's room where each of us took turns holding him, stroking him and crying while he died.

I had never had that experience before. At first, it seemed cruel to me to subject the parents to holding their dying baby. It took only the first few seconds of my turn to hold the child to realize the wisdom of the experience.

He was not a fetus or an "it." He was a real person, worthy of love and worthy of grief because he was dying. It felt good to hold him and cry and tell his parents how beautiful he was. The mother and father unwrapped him, admired each finger and toe, and gave him the only caresses they would ever be able to give.

I talked to those parents several times over the next months. They mourned their son in an appropriate way, but they were also proud of him. He was theirs. They had touched him. He had touched them.

I had touched him, too, and been touched by him. In some way I will never understand fully, I am a better minister and a more compassionate person because of that baby who lived in this world only a few hours. I know it happened because we touched.

I'm telling you this in the hope you will be motivated

to touch and be touched, even at those points in your grief recovery when you are most inclined to withdraw.

One of those times is often about the third month after your loss. Another is between the ninth and twelfth months. Another is at or near the eighteenth month.

You may think that touching or hugging is no more appropriate at these times than I did in that hospital. I want you to know it is not only appropriate, it is great for you!

I now close every session of our grief support group by gathering the people in a close circle where we hold hands as we have a prayer. I think the touch is as vital to our well-being as the prayer.

I also find myself hugging widows, widowers, parents who have lost children, those who come for counseling because of divorce and everyone who has suffered a loss and comes to talk about it. I've never met most of them before the occasion. Neither have I been refused or put off.

Dr. Leo Buscaglia has taught that hugs are good medicine for whatever ails us. They can be lifesavers when we are struggling with grief.

Making Peace with Grief

This exercise requires the help of a friend with a pleasant, soothing voice. Its purpose is to help you become more at peace with your grief and feel more free to open the doors to a new life. You will need a cassette tape recorder and a blank tape.

Ask your friend to record the following message, reading it exactly as it is written. The narrator should speak in a soothing voice at a moderate rate of speed. Wherever three dots appear (...) it means to be silent for about three seconds before going on. The easiest way to time the silence is to count one-and-two-and-three.

Please take a moment to get relaxed. Sit upright in a

comfortable chair with your feet on the floor and your hands held loosely in your lap. Take off your shoes, remove your glasses, and loosen any tight clothing. Be sure you will not be interrupted by the telephone or other distractions.

The narrator will record this message, which you will play back on the recorder:

Please focus your attention on your breathing. Notice how breathing slowly and rhythmically helps you relax...take a few deep breaths...very good...

Now take what we will call a peaceful breath. It's a special kind of deep breath that will tell your body and mind it's time to be at peace. The peaceful breath is taken like this: Breathe out all of the air from your lungs. Inhale slowly through your nose to a count of eight...blow the breath forcefully out through your mouth.

You will note a sensation of tingling after two or three peaceful breaths...that is your sign that you are relaxing deep inside.

Continue to breathe slowly and deeply; breathing in through your nose and out through your mouth. As you do this close your eyes, if you have not already done so...good...now, with your eyes closed, turn your eyes as far to the left as you can, as though you were going to look out your left ear. Keep looking to the left as hard as you can...you may notice that your eye muscles and eyelids have become quite tense...

That's good because I want you to experience the difference between tension and peacefulness. When I count to three, allow your eyes to come back to the front and feel the tension disappear one...two...three...

Feel the soothing peacefulness around your eyes and in

the back of your neck, continue to breathe slowly and deeply...in through your nose, out through your mouth...

Begin to relax all the muscles in your face...around your eyes...in your cheeks...your forehead...your scalp...down to your mouth and chin...you may find your mouth dropping open a bit, that's fine...keep breathing in the same manner, in through your nose, out through your mouth...

Allow your neck muscles to relax...your head tipping forward...you are feeling the relaxation and peacefulness moving to your shoulders...across your back...down to the middle of your back...down to your lower back...

Allow this same peacefulness to flow through your arms to your hands and finger...down each leg and into your feet and toes. Continue to breathe slowly and deeply in through your nose, out through your mouth.

You may become aware of your heartbeat...some people say they feel or hear the blood moving in their arteries. Whatever you are feeling is your body's way of being relaxed and at peace...

Start back at the top of your head and do a peacefulness check list...can you find any place where you are still holding tension?...If so, allow that tension to leave...

As you continue to be relaxed and at peace...the most peaceful you have felt in a long time...concentrate again on your breathing...say to yourself with each exhale, more relaxed...

When you are fully relaxed...take time to enjoy the feeling...allow your body to enjoy the sense of peacefulness...let it into your stomach and intestines...

As you are in this very peaceful, relaxed state, allow your grief to join you, it is not the hurtful, painful thing it was...but a natural part of life...you are at peace with your grief as you are with your natural body. Continue your breathing...

Allow your imagination to create a new life for you as you would like it to be in the future...see all the possibilities for you. Focus on your wish for yourself, as you breathe, tell yourself with every breath "I will fulfill my dream"...add anything else you want to say to yourself...

As you end this exercise you will find that you are refreshed as if you have had a restful sleep. You will be relaxed and yet full of energy, you will have a new sense of well being and a new resolve for your life...

You can come back to this very peaceful state anytime you want to by using your peaceful breathing...now, breathing in an easy, normal way, as I count backwards from five to one, you will open your eyes and be fully alert...five...four...three...two...one.... Very good!

You can play this tape for yourself as often as you want. It is the most effective anytime after the ninth month after your loss.

By the time you reach the point of opening new doors for your life, you not only deserve the right to a sense of peacefulness, but also to "spoil" yourself just a bit.

The following suggestions are given to help you take care of yourself. Your imagination may add others to the list.

It's Okay to Live Again

There are some things you can do that are relatively simple, but which carry strong symbolic images of opening new doors:

❖ *Change your hairstyle to something quite different. Make it 100 percent your choice.*

❖ *Have yourself color-draped. This means having a
   skilled person help you choose the best colors for
   your skin tone and hair. Buy some new clothes in
   your best color.*

❖ *Go on a trip you have wanted to take, but couldn't
   because of responsibilities you no longer have.*

❖ *Remodel one room in your house to suit you.
   Sometimes just paint or wallpaper and a few
   accessories can do wonders.*

❖ *Change your mealtime routine, including the time.
   Many widowed persons find that sitting in their
   spouse's place at the table eases the loneliness.*

[1] Earl Grollman. *Time Remembered.* Boston: Beacon Press, 1984.

16

Your Own
Best Friend

Completing the journey

NOBODY LIKES TO LOSE. Losing always hurts, whether it is a little loss and a little hurt or something equal to the death of your child and a great big hurt.

If you are a normal, healthy person, you want to be a winner. You grew up liking success stories. You were taught to believe bigger is best, more is better and getting is much more fun than losing.

Somewhere along the way you had a minor loss. It was one of those disappointments that can "ruin" your life for at least 48 hours. A well-meaning friend asked, "What did you do to deserve that?" You were pretty sure you must have done something.

Now you have had a major loss. It has impacted your

life for more than a year. Grief has become your constant companion. It has drained your emotions and robbed you of joy. You don't deserve the suffering you have already been through.

You have experienced grief for only one reason. You are alive. You don't deserve the pain or exhaustion, the emptiness, sadness or frustration. I hope you know by now that God did not will your loss. There is not some divine justice system that has punished you for your mistakes.

You are a human being. As long as you are alive, you will experience loss from time to time. Some losses will be small ones and you will soon forget them. Others will change the course of your life.

When you pass the anniversary date of a major loss in your life, there is at least one good thing to say: *You made it!* This seems especially true when your grief is due to death or divorce.

It is finally up to you whether your major losses destroy you or help you grow into a stronger, better person. No one can make you grow through loss, but nothing can keep you from it. When you say, "I made it through this year," you will be acknowledging the greatest accomplishment of your life.

Somewhere between the first and second anniversaries of your loss you will discover a new best friend—yourself.

You have been in the depths. You have faced the worst experiences in your life. You have endured more emotional pain for longer than you ever dreamed you could. You have made decisions that a few months earlier were impossible. In the midst of your own hurt, you have reached out to others who were also grieving.

Now you are beginning to look at the possibilities of a new life. You didn't ask for a new life. You didn't want it. But now that it's here you will make the most of it. It seems to offer joys of its own.

In spite of the ongoing loneliness, you are regaining your balance in life. You now know that you are a remarkable person after all.

Having gone through the most difficult places along the way of grief recovery, you know yourself better than you ever did before. As you build your new life after loss, you need to be especially aware of your strengths and weaknesses.

This exercise should help you identify both more clearly.

Best Friend—Worst Enemy

Divide a sheet of 8-1/2" x 11" paper in half vertically by folding it or drawing a line from top to bottom.

On the left side at the top write "Worst Enemy." On the right side write "Best Friend."

Now reflect on the following statements:

❖ *There is some way in which each of us is our own worst enemy.*

❖ *Likewise, there is some way in which each of us is our own best friend.*

or

❖ *As our own worst enemy we create inner conflicts and make it more difficult to do the things we want or need to do.*

❖ *As our own best friend we bring special skills, gifts and qualities to whatever we are doing.*

On the left side of the paper, list the ways in which you are your own worst enemy.

On the right side, list the ways in which you are your own best friend.

Examine both lists. In what ways can your "best friend" help your "worst enemy?"

Could your worst-enemy traits be helped by a professional counselor? If so, seek that help. Share your lists with your grief support group, clergy or counselor.

As you continue to work through your loss and grief, the tasks before you in the second year will not be as crushing as those behind you. Your most difficult period of time will probably be somewhere around the eighteenth month when some of the old restlessness and impatience may return. As I said before, it won't last. You now also have your newly found best-friend self to help you past this bump in your road to recovery.

If you are recovering from the death of your spouse or a divorce, most of your energies will be devoted to finding ways to shake off the loneliness. Other major losses can leave you with the same task.

Here is a three-word formula for accomplishing this task: *Release...Reorient...Reconnect.*

Release

It is painful to release the emotional ties to that part of your life that has been lost, but you will never fully recover your balance until you do.

It may seem disloyal or sinful to even think about another person after your spouse has died. You may feel guilty when you first begin to enjoy life again.

Your load of disillusionment after a broken marriage may be overwhelming.

It's rough to let go of sentimental attachments to the place where you spent a significant portion of your life.

Nevertheless, this letting go of the past is crucial to moving on to a future life after your loss.

One image that has helped many widowed persons is to pretend the circumstances are reversed. That is, pretend you are the one who has died. If that were the case and you were aware of your spouse's grief, what would you wish for him or her? Would you wish for a lifetime of sadness, depression and loneliness? Not hardly. The two of you have spent years trying to care for one another. You would wish for your spouse to be happy again. Try to imagine your spouse wishing the same for you.

Think about your loss. Is it time for you to release your emotional attachment to whomever or whatever was lost? To the marriage that is never going to be fulfilled? To a stage of life in which you found special meaning? To some other loss?

Rhonda and Bill had both been married before. They were good for each other during the brief time of their marriage before he died of cancer. She took care of him at home until the end, using her professional nursing skills to allow him to die with dignity.

Alan and Margaret lived in the same community. They had shared life together for more than 40 years before she, too, died of cancer. Her deterioration was extremely difficult for Alan to accept. He called in hospice volunteers who helped with nursing and gave him much needed moral support. I was holding hands with both of them when she died.

In time, Alan and Rhonda were able to come to the point of realizing they had done everything they could for their loved ones. It was time to let go and move on. I'll always remember the day Alan called to say he and Rhonda wanted to be married. I have never enjoyed performing a wedding more than that one.

To release your attachment doesn't mean to forget or to deny the importance of that part of your life. It doesn't mean you do not love your deceased child or spouse or parent. It means you understand this person is not going to be a part of your present life, but will live only in your memories. You are going to release your attachment so you can move on to open new doors to life for yourself.

The exercises titled, "Writing a Letter of Good-bye" and "Making Peace with Grief" found in Chapter 15 will help you make this release.

Reorient

The next step is giving yourself permission to begin reorienting your life in new directions.

You will not overcome loneliness by *thinking* about solutions. You will not release an attachment to the past by *waiting* for that attachment to subside.

You overcome loneliness by becoming concerned about other people. Once you discover that you are your own best friend, you can share your friendship with other people. You don't just think about it, you do it.

Those people I know who have done the most to eliminate loneliness from their lives after a major loss are the most involved in helping other bereaved people, community service, devotion to family members and developing new friendships.

Releasing your attachment to the past is also a "doing" behavior. You do your releasing by reorienting your attachments to the present.

For a widow or widower, that might mean a new relationship with a person of the opposite sex. For the parent who has lost a child, it might mean focusing attention on another child in the family, having a baby or adopting a child. In a new city, it means developing loyalties to local sports teams, joining civic groups and getting to know the special features of that community.

The exercise in Chapter 15 titled "It's Okay to Live Again" is a sample of beginning to reorient to a new life.

Another good approach is to think of something you wanted to do before your loss, but could not. Do that thing now.

Susan always wanted to go on a rafting trip through the Grand Canyon. Her husband, Jim, would have no part of it. The subject was the source of more than a few family fights. When Jim got cancer Susan forgot all about the raft and the river. She devoted all of her energies to Jim and their remaining time together.

About 14 months after Jim's death, Susan took their two sons on a river trip through the Grand Canyon. It was a difficult decision for her and she had moments of tears and sadness during the trip. But it was the turning point in her grief recovery. She has now gone back to school, has a good job and recently had her first date, much to her sons' amusement.

Richard and Janna were married for ten stormy years. They were in counseling almost from the beginning, but to no avail. Whatever else they could do in life, they could not seem to be nice to each other. They tried separating, but felt so strongly drawn to each other that they moved back together again. They fought over everything, including money, how to raise their child and what to do on Saturday evening.

Finally, they separated again but neither one could seem to initiate a divorce. Even living apart did not keep them from quarreling. In time, each of them began living with another member of the opposite sex. Richard and his new girlfriend had a child, but still he could not break the emotional tie with Janna. His life was in chaos. He used drugs, drank too much alcohol and wound up in trouble for failure to pay taxes.

It was a matter of years until Richard could work through the loss of his marriage to Janna. The day finally came when the divorce was finalized. A few months later, he and Rebecca were married.

With the ties finally broken, Richard was ready to have his life go in a new direction. He paid off his debts, quit using drugs and no longer abused alcohol. The last I heard, he had saved for the down payment on a house.

Whatever your loss, begin to focus your plans on ways to reorient your life in a new direction. Make a list of things you can do now that you could not do before. Make an effort to begin meeting new people. As you do, write down your feelings about the experience.

Reconnect

Reconnecting is the final step. At this point in your life, you have reoriented your emotions to things in the present. You are able to love another person in marriage, if that is a possible alternative for you. You do not feel compelled to visit the grave site of your child, although you may place flowers there on holidays, birthdays and other special dates.

I remember very clearly the occasion almost three years after we moved away from our home state for the first time. From the time we moved, going back to our former state always felt like going home. Our sense of loss was so great we oftentimes shed tears as we crossed the border returning to our new state. This time, almost three years after our move, we realized that returning to our new state now felt like going home. We paused at the border and shed a few tears at the realization, but these were tears of joy.

I can't tell you when you will be ready for another marriage, another child, a different job or a new city. Perhaps you will never choose any of those. The important thing is for you to be able to do these things, if you want to.

When you have released the past, reoriented to the future and reconnected to the present, you will still have problems simply because you are alive, but loneliness will not be one of them.

Loss and Sexuality

If you are widowed or divorced, the issue of sex is a significant factor in your new life after loss.

I find that those who are widowed have a more difficult time talking about sexuality than those who are divorced. A part of this may be the relative ages at which people are widowed or divorced. It is not that widows in their 60s and 70s are not interested in sexual contact. They come from an era when the subject of sex was not discussed in public—and certainly not with their minister!

If you are a woman who has lost her husband to death, you are one of the 10-million widows in the United States. If you are over the age of 30, the chances of your getting married again are no more than one in two. The odds decline rapidly after 50.

There are about twice the number of new widows each year as widowers. Because of this, most older men are married; most older women are not.

After listening to both divorced and widowed people talk, it seems to me that those who are widowed remain celibate longer than those who are divorced. Most of that has to do with the sense of loyalty the widowed person has to his or her deceased spouse. There is also a crazy cultural "rule" in our society that says it is more appropriate for a divorced person to satisfy the desire for intimacy than a widowed person.

That seems particularly strange when you consider the widowed person has usually come from a relationship where there was more intimacy for a longer time than the divorced person.

Both widowed and divorced persons say that casual sexual encounters are more of a problem than the frustration and loneliness of abstaining.

Finding ways to sublimate sexual energy is helpful for many people. Anything you do that is artistic, creative and social will use some part of your sexuality in creative ways.

A few brave people have said openly that masturbation relieves tension for awhile, but does nothing about the need for talking, holding and caressing with another person.

I urge you to speak out about the problem. It needs talking about in groups and with counselors. There are no easy or pat answers. Being judgmental or moralistic with yourself or others serves no useful purpose.

In her excellent book *The Survival Guide for Widows,* Betty Jane Wylie speaks for widowed and divorced persons when she says, "...the limits of your behavior lie within you and not in the acceptance of society around you."[1]

Money Matters

Money is part of the pathway of your recovery. It may seem like a big jump from sex to money, but the latter, too, is an issue of particular importance to those who are widowed or divorced.

When I asked a group of widows what they would most like to tell young couples to prepare them for the loss of a mate, they responded unanimously with concerns about money matters.

If you are widowed or divorced, your level of income has probably declined. If you are a woman, you may have had to find a job for the first time in years. If you are a divorced man with children, you have learned the facts of child support and keeping two residences.

My widowed friends would tell you to take a class in bookkeeping if your deceased spouse kept the checkbook and paid the bills. My divorced friends who are women would tell you, if you are a woman, to build your own line of credit as soon as you can. Make a small purchase you can easily afford and pay it off promptly.

The chances are you need to know more about budgeting and the use of credit cards than you have before. With all the emotional upheaval and trauma of working through grief, the last thing you need is a financial problem.

Nutrition and Your New Life

Nutrition and physical fitness are vital resources to your recovery. Far too little is said about the roles of food and exercise in grief recovery. The more I learn about the importance of these factors, the more I understand why some people are able to handle their grief so much better than others.

Hal came to see me because he was depressed. He was not adjusting well to career setbacks and personal disappointments. He had been to psychologists and psychiatrists. He had taken medication for depression and been in group therapy for social maladjustment. None of it was helping. He was feeling worse.

Knowing the highly skilled nature of the treatment he had already received, I didn't want to see Hal. I tried to refer him to a psychologist, but he refused. I made an appointment with him not knowing what to try next.

When Hal came in and we began to talk, something he said triggered my interest in his diet. He was a bit shaken that I wanted to talk about the things he ate instead of his emotional problems. He was more shaken when I asked him to see a local nutritionist before we talked further.

The next day he called me in an excited and hopeful voice. Testing had shown he was a suffering from hypoglycemia—low blood sugar. In extreme cases it can dramatically affect moods.

That was surely the case with Hal. By changing his diet, his depression was gone in less than two weeks. His ability to relate with others returned to normal. He was able to work at adjusting to his losses with a new energy and determination. None of the former problems have re-curred.

Hal could have gone through therapy for years, taken medication and still watched his self-esteem sink steadily lower. All he needed to begin a whole new life was a change in the foods he was eating.

It is as important for you to pay attention to your nutrition throughout the length of your grief recovery as it was for Hal. You may not have a blood-sugar problem, but what you are eating and what you are *not* eating can have an impact on your energy level and ability to cope with the stress of the grieving process.

Caffeine and alcohol are stimulants and will not help you handle the stress of grief. Getting all the needed nutrients from the food you eat is one of the most positive things you can do for yourself. It will be more difficult to assure that you get all the important nutrients if your diet includes large quantities of high-fat or high-sugar foods. See Appendix B for more detailed nutrition guidelines.

One of the best investments you can make as you do your grief work is to consult a nutritional expert. Ask about the right things to eat and the foods you should avoid.

Physical Fitness

I also urge you to get whatever amount of physical exercise you can tolerate. Walking is one of the best exercises and a great resource for combating depression.

It's always a good idea to have a check-up by your doctor before beginning any strenuous exercise program.

Most cities have health spas or clubs. If you can afford the cost, it makes an effective social as well as fitness contribution to your stamina for grief work.

Getting on with Life

You can be your own best friend as you make your way along the pathway to grief recovery. That's one of the great discoveries of the journey from loss to life.

All the exercises I have given you are ways you can help yourself regain a zest for living and a deep sense of happiness. It isn't easy and it doesn't come quickly. But, you can emerge from the depths of your loss as one who is on top of life.

One day you will sense it is time to leave the past and get on with the present and the future. When that day comes you will have completed the journey and finished the work. You will be a whole person again.

[1] Betty Jane Wylie. *The Survival Guide for Widows.* New York: Ballantine Books, 1984.

17

Preparing
for Loss

A new dimension in wholeness

THERE IS NO WAY to prepare for the loss of a loved
one! You have heard this said many times. You may have
said it yourself. Actually, most of us don't think there is a
way to prepare for any of life's major losses.

However, regardless of how many of us believe there
is no way to prepare for loss, *it isn't true!*

If you have not experienced a major loss, you need to
know you are not helpless before the prospect of such an
inevitable event in your life. You can prepare for losses
including the death of a spouse, child, parent, sibling or
friend, divorce, moving to a new city or state, retiring from
work, children leaving home, major surgery, the loss of a
job and any other major change in life.

Having had a major loss once doesn't give you an assurance there won't be more. Even if you weren't prepared the first time, there is no reason not to be prepared now.

Marge, whose husband had been ill for many years, described her anxiety about his declining health. She said, "I feel like an ant in the path of an avalanche. Everything is out of control and rushing toward me. All I can do is wait for his death because I know it's coming. I don't talk about it because I don't know of anything I can do about it. I wait in silence."

Breaking the Silence

The first thing you can do to prepare for loss is break the conspiracy of silence about it. There is a certain superstition many people have that says, "If you talk about something bad, it will happen." I think most of us know that is a silly notion—but we still keep silent.

A widow said to me, "Bill and I never talked about death. He always believed if we talked about it, one of us would die." They didn't talk about death, but he died anyway at the age of 80. His widow was left with many things she had never told him and a deep sense of guilt to compound the pain of her grief.

Two years after his death she could no longer keep up the many plants and greenery he had planted around their home. She had meant to tell him that she couldn't do gardening like him because of her arthritis, but never got around to it. She was afraid he would be upset because she was planning for his demise. Finally, she had the plants removed. She went through months of deep depression afterwards because she was certain she had failed to meet his expectations of her.

Preparing for Loss Is Preparing for Life

Preparing for loss is not a morbid activity. It is not to become a pessimist about life, but an optimist who is also a realist. It is not to say, *Bad things will not happen to me.* It is to say, *I can get through any loss in my life.*

You will not avoid the pain of grief or the steps through grief described in this book. I know of no way to get under, over or around the heartache of a major loss. Preparing for loss is strengthening yourself for the task of taking charge of your grief. It isn't easy or fun. But it is necessary and possible.

As soon as you decide there are things you can do to prepare for life's inevitable losses, you have begun to take charge of your own destiny. This can be a new experience in itself. You will no longer feel as vulnerable or helpless. The unforeseen, unpredictable circumstances of life won't have the same power to terrify you.

As I write these very words, the telephone has interrupted me with a call from a family whose three-year-old daughter was just killed in an accident. Tragic events do happen in this world! You can't always avoid them. You can be prepared to face the grief that follows such losses.

Preparing Your Body for Grief

Physical health is as important as mental health in working your way through a major loss. Good nutrition, physical exercise, adequate fluids and sufficient rest are all important *during* grief. They are equally important as a means of *preparing* for grief. Whatever your age or physical limitations might be, you can achieve an optimum level of health *for you* with very little work.

I suggest checking with your doctor to find the best dietary plan and level of exercise for your particular situation. Don't wait until you experience a loss to take care of yourself.

Nobody Does Grief Work Perfectly

In my experience, those who have unrealistic expectations of themselves do not do well at handling grief and loss. If you are one of those who always demands just a little bit more of yourself, you will add unnecessary frustration and guilt to your grief. Nobody does grief work perfectly. It is a time of slipping and sliding, of three steps forward and three back, of doing your best and discovering it wasn't enough.

To prepare for loss, search out any unrealistic standards you have for yourself and change your expectations. Learn to be more patient with yourself before you have to face the challenge of grief.

Even if you have not already experienced a major loss, work through some of the exercises in this book. Ask yourself how you think you would respond to the death of a loved one, relocating to another area far from familiar sights and faces or a divorce. Getting in touch with your feelings about the possibility of such events is a way of beginning to prepare for losses that are unavoidable.

Loss and grief are not enjoyable experiences for anyone, but they happen to all of us at some time and usually more than once. You *can* prepare for loss in the simple but important ways I have outlined here.

Perhaps the greatest benefit of preparing is not what preparation does for life *after* loss, but what it does for life *before* loss.

The final thing I want you to do before you lay this book down is take a fantasy trip. As you read the words that follow, allow your imagination to take you on the journey it describes.

The Secret Box

You are in a meadow. It is a beautiful green place with wavy grass and a scattering of colorful flowers. The sky is blue overhead with just a few puffs of white clouds. (Close your eyes for a moment and create this scene in your imagination. When you are ready to go on, open your eyes and continue reading.)

You walk through the meadow and come to a crystal-blue lake. There is a short sandy beach, so you take off your shoes and feel the grainy sand, warmed by the bright sunlight.

You walk across the beach to the water and wade in a short distance. Now you can feel the coolness of the water as compared to the warmth of the sand. It is very pleasant. (If you like, take a moment to close your eyes again and let your imagination take you into this scene. When you are ready to continue, open your eyes and read on.)

This is the amazing part. You walk farther into the water, feeling it come up around your knees, then your waist. The lake bottom is very smooth and sandy with no rocks or weeds. You continue to walk into the cool, clear water as it rises to your chest, then your neck.

The great thing about a fantasy is that we are not limited by the usual constraints of our physical world. So, you continue walking into the water until you are under the surface! Wonder of wonders, you can breathe the water as though it were air, and you do not float. The sights around you are beautiful and you feel very secure and elated. The water is cool and refreshing around you and, as you breathe it, you know why the fish are so energetic. (You may want to lay the book down again for a moment and close your eyes to get the full effect. When you are ready, go on reading.)

As you walk deeper, the light grows dimmer, except for a very strong beam of sunlight that pierces the water at the very center of the lake. As you approach that place, you see a small box lying on the sand. It is shaped like a small pirate's chest, made of dark wood and has a brass handle.

You pick up the box and open it. The light from the sunbeam illuminates the contents so you can see them clearly. You know what is in the box. (Close your eyes so that your imagination can see it very distinctly. When you are sure you know what is there, open your eyes and continue reading.)

You close the box and carry it with you out of the water and up onto the shore. As you walk toward the meadow, a figure appears. It is a man. He walks toward you. Though he is a stranger, you are drawn to him. He smiles and you know you have nothing to fear.

As you draw near to the stranger, you are surprised because you feel completely at ease. You say nothing and the man says nothing. You are standing very close and you just look into each other's eyes.

Without a word, you hold out the box and the man reaches out and takes it. You look at each other for a minute longer, then he nods and you turn and walk away.

You walk back through the meadow feeling the warm sun on your back and a gentle breeze around you. You walk more lightly than you have in a long time. You know inside that life is really good after all. And you are healed.

When you are finished with this story, lay the book down. Stand up and walk around for a minute or two. Notice that you feel a little bit lighter than you did when you began reading.

Life after Loss

Earlier, I suggested that talking with someone who had recovered from grief was like talking to an adventurer. I said those who conquered grief talk more about what they have found than what they have lost. Their lives reflect the events of the past, but are focused on the future. Death and loss do not dominate their thoughts. They have a sense of joy that is more solid than most of us because they know there is nothing life can deal that they can't handle. They are compassionate people. They have more patience than most folks. They have a reverence for life and a deep appreciation for human relationships.

It is my hope and prayer that when you have made your way through your grief as you have through this book, others will think that talking to you is like talking to an adventurer.

May your life after loss be full and rewarding.

[1] Nina H. Donnelley. *I Never Know What to Say, How to help your family and friends cope with tragedy*. New York: Ballantine Books, 1987.

A p p e n d i x   A

Words that
Describe Feelings

IT IS NOT EASY TO PUT FEELINGS into words. The task becomes more difficult when our feelings are very strong either positively or negatively. We commonly say, "The sunset was beautiful beyond words," or "I love you more than words can say." We also say, "There are no words to describe the pain I feel because of his death."

To be able put our feelings into words is important even though it is difficult. Describing our feelings of grief is an act of healing.

The primary reason we have so much trouble talking about our feelings is the language we use. We commonly say "I feel" when, in fact, we are saying "I think." We say "I feel that the best way to do this is..." That sentence describes a thought, not a feeling. The misuse of the phrase "I feel" has created a block to expressing our feelings easily.

The simplest way to be sure you are describing feelings instead of thoughts is to see if substituting the phrase "I think" for "I feel" changes the meaning of what you are saying. If you are describing your feelings, changing the phrase will not make sense. For instance, to say, "I feel miserable and in the dumps because of my loss" makes sense, but to say, "I *think* miserable and in the dumps…" does not. The first sentence accurately describes your feelings.

However, if you say, "I feel my experience of loss is the worst thing to happen to me," you can change the statement to "I *think* my experience of loss is the worst thing to happen to me" and still make sense. In this case you would not be describing your feelings, but instead, a thought you have about your loss.

The following words describe feelings. As you are writing in your journal or working through the various exercises in the book, refer to this list often. Find the best word to describe the feeling you are trying to describe.

HAPPY	ANGRY	SAD
contented	outraged	sour
relaxed	irritated	miserable
serene	furious	bleak
peaceful	cross	unhappy
joyous	annoyed	dismal
glad	tantrum	dreary
cheerful	burn	mournful
merry	seethe	discouraged
exhilarated	infuriated	depressed
elated	enraged	in the dumps
jubilant	bitter	flat
carefree	fuming	melancholy
lighthearted	wrathful	forlorn
ecstatic	frustrated	joyless

FEARFUL
fearful
shaky
panicky
hysterical
shocked
horrified
anxious
scared
petrified
alarmed

TENSE
taut
uptight
tense
weak
immobilized
paralyzed
stretched
hollow
breathless

HURT
injured
offended
afflicted
aching
crushed
tortured
pained
suffering
lonely
distressed
cold

COURAGEOUS
encouraged
confident
secure
reassured
bold
brave
determined
proud
daring

EAGER
fascinated
creative
earnest
excited
keen
avid
sincere
intrigued
inquisitive

DOUBTFUL
unbelieving
suspicious
uncertain
wavering
hopeless
powerless
hesitant
defeated
pessimistic

A   p   p   e   n   d   i   x   B

The Role of Nutrition in Grief Recovery

THE ROLE OF NUTRITION in grief recovery does not get the attention it deserves. A diet complete in all the necessary nutrients is crucial to maintaining your health during the long and stressful time it takes to work through a major loss.

Maintaining an appropriate weight is the first step. We each respond to stress differently. Some people tend to eat more when stressed, and consequently gain weight, while others become disinterested in food and therefore lose weight. In either instance, if the gain or loss is more than 10 percent of your usual weight, it is likely that you will be lacking essential nutrients, and your energy to cope with stress will be decreased.

To help save energy, prepare simple meals using casseroles and one-dish meals or choose from entrées and dinners that are well-balanced but not too high in fat or salt. Use your blender, crock-pot, microwave or toaster oven to save effort. Let friends or relatives help if they offer to prepare a dish or meal for you. Occasionally take advantage of a local restaurant's home delivery service. Use whatever means works for you. Just be sure not to skip meals or rely on only a few foods for all your nutrition. A wide variety of foods and adequate quantities are the cornerstones of a good diet.

Fluids are also very important. Your body needs water to keep all the systems working properly and to keep essential nutrients in proper balance. Beverages that are high in caffeine or contain alcohol can act as diuretic and therefore lead to further dehydration. Just plain water is the best fluid you can take!

The following guidelines are provided for your reference. They are sound, common-sense points that will assure you of a diet which will help, not hinder, your recovery, and that will be good for you for the rest of your life. If you have special dietary needs or desire more detailed nutrition information, a Registered Dietician is best qualified to help. Your local hospital is an excellent resource.

Dietary Guidelines

1. Establish a regular schedule for meals and snacks and stick to it.

2. Drink at least eight glasses (eight ounces each) of water a day.

3. Use the following food groups and quantities as a daily guide:

Wholegrain breads and cereals — 4-6 servings
Fruits and vegetables — 4-6 servings
Low-fat dairy products — 2 servings
Meat and meat substitutes — 4-6 ounces

4. Smaller, more frequent meals may be easier to eat than three large meals. Make sure your snacks are nutritious and that your total daily intake is still adequate.

5. Plan your meals and snacks in advance to ensure balanced, adequate meals, and to make shopping less time- and energy-consuming.

6. Use iron-rich foods more often, including lean meats, seafood, fortified bread and cereals, leafy green vegetables, dried fruits, nuts, dried peas and beans.

7. Carbohydrates are most easily digested by your body and are its best source of energy to help you overcome the fatigue that is often associated with grief. Include at least one serving of complex carbohydrates (not sugars) at each meal, such as bread, crackers, cereal, pasta, potatoes, rice, and dried peas and beans.

8. All the needed vitamins and minerals can be obtained from the food you eat if the recommended quantities are included daily. If your intake is not adequate or is adequate only sporadically, a supplement may be appropriate. However, large quantities of some vitamins and minerals can be harmful. Consult a Registered Dietician if you feel you need supplements.

9. Once a month write down everything you eat for three days and compare your daily totals with the recommended daily amounts from each food group.

10. Weigh yourself once a week, preferably first thing in the morning. If you begin to see significant changes, talk with your physician or a Registered Dietician.

Sample Menu

Breakfast
Citrus fruit or juice
Wholegrain toast with small amount of margarine
Egg, egg substitute or reduced-fat cheese
Low-fat milk, decaffeinated coffee or herbal tea

Lunch

Sandwich: wholegrain bread, roll or bagel; mustard or reduced-fat mayonnaise; lean meat, fish or cheese; lettuce, tomato, onion, peppers, etc.
Bean salad or coleslaw
Fresh or canned fruit
Decaffeinated, non-alcoholic beverage

Dinner

Lean meat, skinless poultry or fish; broiled, baked or poached
Potato with skin, brown rice or wholewheat pasta
Dark green or yellow vegetable
Fruit salad
Low-fat pudding or yogurt
Decaffeinated, non-alcoholic beverage

Snacks

Pretzels or popcorn
Wheat crackers or bagel chips
Graham crackers or plain cookies
Dried or fresh fruit
Raw vegetables
Low-fat milk, yogurt or cheeses
Nuts, nut butters, seeds or granola (although these are higher in fat)

Note: Thanks to Sister Joneen Keuler, R.D., clinical dietician at Tucson Medical Center in Tucson, Arizona, for the material in Appendix B and a review of nutrition-related comments throughout the text.

A p p e n d i x   C

Forming a
Support Group

FORMING A GRIEF SUPPORT GROUP is a fairly easy thing to do. Because major loss is such a universal human experience, you will have little difficulty finding people in your community who are willing to participate.

One of your first tasks will be to decide what the focus of the group will be. Will it be just for widows and widowers? Or, will it also include those who have lost children, parents or other loved ones? Will it focus only on the grief that follows death? Do you want to address the needs of divorced persons? Do you want the group limited to people in your church or neighborhood?

If you are going to be the one to form the group, reflect on your own situation and needs and start from there.

Be assured that once you have penetrated people's initial anxiety about meeting with strangers, you will find a positive response.

Churches, synagogues, clubs, fraternal organizations, PTA groups and your own circle of friends are all good places to seek participants for a support group.

There are several ways to call a group together. The following have all been used successfully:

1. Ask your minister, priest or rabbi to publish a notice in their newsletter about the formation of a support group. Ask people to submit their names. Include your name and telephone number for additional information.

2. Put a notice in a club or fraternal group's newsletter. Offer to let the group meet at your home or arrange another place.

3. Consult a local psychologist about offering a six- to eight-session series on grief and loss. Often, a counselor or psychologist will do it free of charge for potential referrals.

4. Talk to friends about getting together to support each other in times of loss and to share past experiences.

5. Publish a notice in your local newspaper or post flyers in markets, drugstores and other public display places announcing the formation of the group.

Whatever approach you take, be specific about the group's purpose, length of time it will meet and cost, if any.

It is always good to put an end date on the initial series of meetings. This encourages people to be regular in attendance and provides a "safety valve" in case anyone has emotional problems that are too severe for the group to handle.

Have each participant get a copy of this book to use as a guide.

Groups should consist of at least four people, but no more than 10 without a trained leader.

Unless a professional counselor is called in, it is important that whoever calls the group together lead the first series of meetings.

If the group is not lead by a trained professional, its purpose will be different. *Untrained persons should not attempt therapy with members of the group.* However, providing a setting where people can freely share experiences and feelings and find a network of others who care is extremely helpful. A self-help format requires only that the leader understand the principles of grief recovery explained in this book.

The fundamental principles for a self-directed group are these:

❖ *Feelings are neither right nor wrong. The leader must be as accepting of anger and frustration as of hopefulness and joy.*

❖ *It takes a long time to work through loss and grief. Review the steps of grief recovery in Chapter Four.*

Session One

The first session is especially important. People often feel uncomfortable and anxious about what is going to take place. It is important for the leader to establish an atmosphere of relaxed security. If a professional counselor is not present, there are several ways to do this:

1. Provide a comfortable, "homey" setting. Soft lights (not dim), comfortable chairs arranged in a circle, easy-to-read name tags and isolation from other distracting noises all help to establish the kind of setting that is needed.

2. Children should not be present because they are too distracting. Childcare may have to be provided at a different location.

3. Refreshments, if any, should be restricted to light beverages until the session is completed. Alcoholic beverages can be a problem. Avoid them.

4. At least one full box of tissues should be within easy reach at every session. (I keep five full boxes on hand and deliberately set one out on a table or empty chair as each session begins).

Begin by reminding everyone of the group's purpose. Have each person give his or her name and tell why he or she is coming to the group. Everyone should describe the loss they have experienced in as much detail as they wish. Encourage them to use the names of deceased or divorced persons.

It is important at this point of the group's life together that others just listen and not give any advice. It is common to hear repeatedly, "I thought I was the only one who felt like that." It helps if the leader calls attention to the common ground of the group's experiences.

The main goal of the meeting is for people to tell their stories and to know they have been listened to and understood.

The group should meet for no more than 90 minutes and should end on time. Using prayer at the closing is a matter of personal choice. If prayer is used, it should be short, affirming and not "preachy."

It is good to create a roster of the group and have a printed list of names, addresses and telephone numbers ready for each participant at the second meeting.

Session Two

The setting should be prepared again as it was for the first meeting.

Be sure the box of tissues is clearly visible and easily reachable.

Use name tags again if group members do not already know each other or if new persons are joining.

Have each member of the original group introduce himself to the newcomers and briefly tell his losses. Then the new people are welcomed to share their stories.

Present the Four Key Facts about Grief as described in Chapter Six. Take time for group discussion on each one and how various members are experiencing it. Don't rush! You may take up the entire evening with just the first one: The Way Out of Grief is Through It, Because There is No Way Around It.

It is quite possible that tears will flow during the discussion. It is important to always affirm to the group the appropriateness of crying.

If time remains, ask for people to describe the particular problems they have faced in the past week. Keep in mind that where people are in their grief process will determine the focus of their sharing.

In closing, ask people to identify themselves if they are willing to be called at home by others in the group. Urge group members to put a mark by these names on their rosters. The support that group members sometime give each other in these informal, between-sessions contacts, is often as helpful as the meetings themselves. It is not unusual to see lasting friendships develop in this way.

Session Three

Begin the session by asking if anyone has anything to share with the group. There may be a tendency to sidetrack onto issues not directly related to the individual's grief recovery. For instance, if someone is in the stage of blaming others for the loss, that person may take up excessive time talking about those others instead of his or her own feelings. If this occurs, it is the task of the leader to bring the focus of conversation back to the immediate experience of the group members. Do it gently.

Pass out paper and pencils.

Have the group diagram their moods over the past year according to the instructions on page 78. Ask them to describe their feelings at the moment in terms of a color, taste, smell, touch, and sound.

Have each person write an answer to this question: If I could change one thing in my life right now, what would it be?

Give everyone adequate time to do all of the above assignments. When the answers have been recorded, go around the group and discuss one question at a time. Try to draw out feelings and more detailed descriptions if anyone gives only superficial, brief responses.

Before closing give each person the following "home-work" assignment:

❖ *Purchase a stenographer's notepad and label it "journal."*

❖ *Record each day for the next week:*
   a significant event that happened;
   the person who was most important to me today;
   feelings of which I was most aware today;
   plans for tomorrow.

❖ *Note date and time of day of entries at top of page.*

❖ *Bring journal to the group next week.*

Session Four

Begin this and all subsequent sessions with the same invitation to share that was given in Session Three.

Ask for sharing about people's experience with keeping a journal. It is common for some group members to have either "forgotten" (repressed) the assignment or completed only part of it. Be sure to acknowledge that this is okay and they can try again.

Have those who are willing share some portion of their journal entries. You may want to ask them to choose a particular day and share the entries from that day.

Ask the group members to continue keeping a journal for the balance of the group sessions. They should add the following notations:

❖ *Changes I observe happening to me*

❖ *Notes to myself*

As the group moves into more personal sharing, it is normal for some people to report feeling worse at the end of the meeting than they did when they arrived. *Assure participants that this is normal* and a significant sign of growth. It is not a sign of slipping backward, but of moving forward. It is not a negative thing, but a necessary positive thing, even though it is uncomfortable. It will pass and they will feel much better if they stay with the process.

If people drop out at this time, try to maintain contact and help them establish some other base of support.

If any group member seems to manifest the symptoms of distorted grief as described on pages 50-52, encourage that person to seek the help of a professional counselor or psychologist.

Close the session in whatever way has become appropriate and effective for your group.

Session Five

After any open sharing, review the following guidelines for growing through loss which are described in some detail in Chapter Seven:

❖ *Believe that your grief has a purpose and an end.*

❖ *Be responsible for your own grief process.*

❖ *Don't be afraid to ask for help.*

❖ *Don't rush it.*

Discuss how group members are experiencing each of these guidelines. Where are they having the most problems? Where do they seem to have a good grasp on their grief?

To close, lead the group in doing the 8-8-8 Breather exercise beginning on page 155. Repeat the sequence several times. When finished with the exercise, join hands in a circle and give each other words of encouragement for the next week.

Session Six

After giving an opportunity for open sharing, ask the group to talk about the positive and negative ways religious faith has affected their grief experience.

It is especially important, when dealing with the subject of religion, that people's individual views and feelings are recognized. Some people are very angry at God. Some cannot express that anger; some will deny it altogether. Others may have abandoned their faith as a result of their grief. Still others will look to their faith as the foundation for trying to put life back together again. You may find people who are convinced that God is punishing them. Others may tell you that God has taken their loved one. Whatever a person's feelings might be, the most helpful thing the group can do is just listen.

Avoid getting into philosophical discussions about the presence of evil in the world, why tragic things happen to good people, or whether God punishes people through grief experiences.

Ask group members to keep their sharing personal and to accept the sharing of others, even if it is quite different from their own experience.

At the close of the session, do the 8-8-8 Breather exercise. Repeat the sequence several times. If the group is open to it, close the meeting by joining hands in a circle and offering a short prayer of gratitude. I ask directly, "Would you be comfortable if we had a prayer before we close?" I find that people will give an honest answer if an open and accepting atmosphere has been established during the session. If some wish to have prayer and others do not, allow those who do not to exercise the option of excluding themselves. The prayer should be brief, positive and hopeful.

Remind everyone to keep writing in their journals on a daily basis. You may want to review the instructions from Session Three.

Session Seven

Begin by asking for people to share something significant from their journal writing of the past week. After all have an opportunity to share, ask if anyone is having problems with forgetfulness.

You can be sure that many are experiencing this. Locking keys in the car, misplacing house keys, forgetting appointments, telephone numbers and people's names are common after a major loss. Assure the group that such behavior is a normal part of the grief experience for many people.

Encourage people to keep an extra set of car keys in a magnetic box somewhere under a fender or have an extra door key kept separately from the rest of their keys. It's a good idea to have a trusted neighbor keep a set of house keys. Even the most familiar and frequently used telephone numbers and addresses should be written down and kept in a visible place.

Ask these additional questions:

❖ *Has anyone here wondered if you are the only one having these kinds of problems with grief?*

❖ *Do you find that routine tasks are more difficult?*

❖ *Do you ever wonder if you are going crazy?*

You will find that most people in the group have experienced all or some of these symptoms of grief. It's called *fragmenting* and it's totally normal in the first three to six months after a major loss. Those who have moved beyond this stage will remember when it happened to them. I have talked with people whose loss was more than five years old and they had never told anyone about the fragmenting symptoms. Just talking about them and discovering that other people experience similar symptoms often helps to lift a heavy weight from the shoulders of bereaved people.

One of the beneficial "spin-offs" of this sharing is the common bond it can create between those who are divorced and those who are widowed. Oftentimes, if widowed and divorced persons are in the same group, there is a certain amount of tension between them. Exercises such as this one help bridge that tension by focusing on the reactions to loss and grief that are common to both.

If time permits after the discussion on forgetfulness, ask the group to talk about any problems they are having with nongrieving people. This is another subject that brings grieving people closer to each other.

Have the group review the section that addresses the subject of relating to non-grievers, pages 162-65.

As a homework assignment for the next week, ask the group to focus on forgiveness in their journal writing.

❖ *Who do you need to forgive for failing to respond to your loss in a helpful way?*

❖ *Is there anyone you blame for your loss?*

❖ *Do you need to forgive yourself for anything?*

Sharing on this forgiveness will open the next session of the group.

Close by joining hands in a circle and having members of the group give expressions of the unity they feel with the others as a result of their experiences together over the past six weeks.

Session Eight

Open the session by asking the group to respond to these questions:

❖ *Who has been a significant person in my life this week?*

❖ *What did this person do for me?*

After this sharing is completed, ask if anyone in the group ever has problems going to sleep or getting up. (By this time in the life of your group, the subject of sleep problems may have already come up).

Have people share their experiences. You may find wide variations between people. Some have no problems with either sleep or feeling fatigued. Others will have problems with both of these symptoms. Again, there is great value for the participants in hearing other people's experience.

This is a good time to review the information on nutrition in Appendix B. Many times, what a person eats and drinks will result in more energy during the day and better rest at night.

Tell the group the following story about Hazel:

Hazel could not sleep after her divorce and subsequent surgery for a leg injury suffered in a fall. She was growing increasingly irritable, performing poorly at work and gaining weight. Her leg was not healing.

She went for counseling to find out what was wrong with her emotionally and spiritually. After a few minutes of gathering information, the counselor asked her to describe what she did during the evening and what food and drink she consumed *after* dinner—which she normally ate about 6:00 p.m..

Hazel reported that she grew increasingly anxious as the evening went on. At first she felt a vague nervousness, but after her failure to fall asleep on a couple of occasions, she focused her anxiety on that.

To relieve the discomfort and to occupy her mind with other things, she would begin working crossword puzzles about 9:00 p.m. She drank hot chocolate and ate cookies while working on the puzzles.

Without realizing what she was doing, Hazel was stimulating her body with sugar and caffeine while she stimulated the analytical portion of her mind with the crossword puzzles. There was no way she was going to be able to fall asleep within hours of that kind of activity and food intake.

The counselor suggested she change the hot chocolate to decaffeinated herbal tea and the cookies to raw vegetables or a dish of oatmeal with warm milk. He also suggested she substitute a book of poetry or photographic artwork for her crossword puzzles.

Within three nights, Hazel had returned to her normal sleep patterns. She also visited a local nutrition counselor for guidance on possible vitamin supplements. It was only a short time later that her leg began to heal.

Focus the balance of sharing on people's response to the story of Hazel and what it says about their own experience.

As a homework assignment, have each person prepare a daily calendar for themselves for the next week. The daytime hours should be divided into three sections: morning, afternoon and evening. Have them list what they plan to do during each of these periods of time for the next day.

The calendar for nighttime hours after their normal bedtime should be listed in half-hour intervals. They should list what they will do during each half-hour of the night until their regular time of rising, should they not be able to go to sleep or wake up in the middle of the night.

I suggest listing tasks that need to be done that the person does not like to do and usually puts off as long as possible.

This schedule should be filled out each day and followed as closely as possible. Announce that the opening sharing for Session Nine will be focused on each person's experiences with the calendar for the week.

Close the group in whatever way has become most comfortable for the participants.

Session Nine

The first order of business for the session is to have everyone report on their experience with the daily calendars. Take enough time for each person to share his or her successes and failures. Assure them that whatever happened, it was okay and they can continue to use the exercise for as long as they wish.

Pass out a clean sheet of lined notebook paper to each person. Dictate the following statement. Ask each person to write it down as you read.

The sadness I feel is a badge of honor. I wear the brokenness of my life at this moment with pride. These expressions of my grief testify to the importance of (each person will fill in the name of person, place or condition that has been lost) to me.

I am willing to feel the full impact of my grief as a final act of tribute and love. I will make my way through this experience and will not run from it.

Signed,
(Your name)

Before anyone signs the statement, take time to talk about how each one feels about it. In what way does each one see his or her grief as a badge of honor? What feelings do people have about signing this statement?

Some members of the group may want to make a change in the statement before signing it. Allow anyone to make whatever changes are necessary to make the statement true for them.

Have each person sign the statement. Then, using tape, post it on a wall where all can see it. Do this one person at a time. As each one posts his or her statement, have them read it aloud, including any changes that have been made.

After all statements are posted, take time to talk about the experience.

The homework assignment for the following week is to write letters to and from one's grief. You will find a full description of this exercise on pages 160-162.

Close the group by having everyone gather their statements from the wall, put them in a pile on a chair and gather around it, holding hands. Join in a short prayer or some other affirmation of what the statements represent.

Session Ten

Begin the session with opportunity for open sharing about significant events of the week.

Ask for people to report on their experience with writing to and from their grief. Those who have brought their letters with them may want to read them to the group.

It is important to affirm anyone who was unable to carry out the assignment. It is not unusual to have several who can't face the task at the present time. If you are accepting of everyone's experience, a valuable discussion can follow, regardless of whether or not the letters were written.

Talk about how people felt as they wrote each letter or found they could not write one or both of them.

When all have shared, have the group lay aside everything they are holding. Tell them the next exercise is one of relaxation as reward for all their hard work.

Everyone should get in a comfortable position with feet flat on the floor, arms and hands in laps and eyes closed. Begin with a few repetitions of the 8-8-8 Breather exercise.

Read aloud the exercise beginning on page 180 titled "Making Peace with Grief." Your vocal tone should be peaceful and soft, but easy to hear. If you are uncomfortable reading the monologue, have someone else record it on a cassette and play it for the group.

When the exercise is completed, take time to talk about individual experiences with it. Remember, no one response is "right." Whatever reaction people have is valid for them and will reflect their own personality and stage of grief.

As a homework assignment, ask the group to keep a daily log of their food intake, using the guidelines found in Appendix B. These logs should be brought to Session Eleven.

Close the session in whatever manner has become most appropriate for your group.

Session Eleven

As you open this session, remind the group that you have only one more session to go. Ask for people to talk about the issues of grief and loss that are most important to them at this time. What is there that each person wants the group to hear before it is disbanded? Remember, as leader, you should be ready to deal with issues of loss during this next to last group session. These issues, too, should be talked about freely.

Call the group's attention to the material found in Appendix B about the role of nutrition in grief recovery. Ask each person to discuss his or her daily log of food intake for the past week. Did everyone keep the log? If not, why not? If it was kept, what was learned from it about each one's nutritional strengths and weaknesses?

If it is possible to get a nutritionist to come to the meeting for this portion of it, that is a real plus.

Next, talk about what each person is doing in the area of physical fitness. Just 45 minutes of brisk walking can do wonders at lifting spirits and easing depression. Urge everyone to have a physical examination if they haven't had one since their loss. This is especially important for those who are four to six months past a major loss experience.

Any program of exercise and fitness should be done with the involvement and direction of each person's doctor.

Close the session in the manner that is most appropriate for your group.

Session Twelve

Plan to have some special refreshments at the close of this final session. Allow time for casual interaction and fellowship before people leave.

Open the session by reminding everyone that it is the last session. Ask for sharing about what people have gained from the sessions and how they feel about its ending.

In most cases, some of the group members will want to go on meeting. You should decide before this session whether or not you wish to continue in the group or as its leader. In any event, it is best to take a break of at least one week before going on.

Another decision that often must be made at this time is whether or not to take in new members to the group. Keep in mind that newcomers will not have gone through the exercises and experiences of the "veteran" group members. In most cases, unless a trained leader is in charge, I think it is best to either disband and start all over again or create a second group for newcomers and go on with those of the original group who wish to continue meeting.

It is very important that no one in the current group is pressured into continuing.

After everyone has shared on the opening subject, ask the group to do the exercise on page 187 titled "Best Friend—Worst Enemy." Share the results of the exercise with each other.

Close the session and the series by doing the exercise beginning on page 202 titled "The Secret Box." You should narrate it rather than having the group read it individually.

When the exercise is completed, gather the group in a circle and express thanks to each other for everyone's support and caring. Close with a short prayer or other affirmative statement.

For Further Reading

Buscaglia, Leo. *The Fall of Freddie the Leaf*. Charles B.
  Slack Inc., 1982.
Cain, Albert. *Survivors of Suicide*. C.C. Thomas, 1972.
Carpenter, Rachel. *A Practical Guide to Prepare for and
  Survive Widowhood*. Carpenter Ventures, 1990.
Clinebell, Howard. *Growth Counseling for Mid-Years
  Couples*. Fortress Press, 1977.
Colgrove, Melba; Harold Bloomfield; Peter McWilliams.
  How to Survive the Loss of a Love. Bantam, 1981.
Davidson, Glen W. *Understanding Mourning*. Augsburg,
  1984.
Diamond, Harvey; Marilyn Diamond. *Fit For Life*. Warner
  Books, 1985.
Donnelley, Nina H. *I Never Know What to Say; How to
  help your family and friends cope with tragedy*.
  Ballantine, 1987.
Fox, Arnold; Barry Fox. *Immune For Life*. Prima
  Publishing, 1990.

Gaffney, Donna. *The Seasons of Grief*. NAL Books, 1988.

Ginsburg, Genevieve. *To Live Again*. Jeremy P. Tarcher, Inc., 1987.

Greteman, Jim. *Coping With Divorce; From grief to healing*. Ave Maria Press, 1981.

Grollman, Earl. *Explaining Death to Children*. Beacon Press, 1967.

_____. *Living When a Loved One Has Died*. Beacon Press, 1977.

_____. *Talking About Death*. Beacon Press, 1990.

_____. *What Helped Me When My Loved Ones Died*. Beacon Press, 1982.

_____. *Time Remembered*. Beacon Press, 1987.

Hausman, Patricia; Judith Benn Hurley. *The Healing Foods*. Dell Publishing, 1989.

Jackson, Edgar. *The Many Faces of Grief*. Abingdon, 1972.

_____. *Understanding Grief*. Abingdon, 1957.

Krantzler, Mel. *Creative Divorce*. Signet Books, 1974.

Kübler-Ross, Elisabeth. *On Death and Dying*. MacMillan, 1969.

_____. *Living With Death and Dying*. MacMillan, 1982.

_____. *Questions and Answers on Death and Dying*. MacMillan, 1974.

_____. *On Children and Death*. MacMillan, 1985.

Kushner, Harold S. *When Bad Things Happen to Good People*. Schocken Books, 1981.

Lindemann, Erich. *Beyond Grief: Studies in Crisis Intervention*. Jason Aronson, Inc., 1979.

Lewis, C.S. *A Grief Observed*. Bantam, 1976.

Lord, Janice Harris. *Beyond Sympathy*. Pathfinder Publishing, 1988.

Lynch, James. *The Broken Heart: The Medical Consequences of Loneliness*. Basic Books, 1977.

Manning, Doug. *Comforting Those Who Grieve*. Harper & Row, 1985.

_____. *Don't Take My Grief Away; What to do when you lose a loved one*. Harper & Row, 1984.

Marshall, Fiona. *Losing a Parent*. Fisher Books, 1993.

Mitchell, Kenneth; Herbert Anderson. *All Our Losses, All Our Griefs: Resources for Pastoral Care*. Westminster Press, 1983.

Nouwen, Henri. *A Letter of Consolation.* Harper & Row, 1982.

O'Connor, Nancy. *Letting Go with Love; The grieving process.* La Mariposa Press, 1984.

Phipps, William. *Death: Confronting the Reality.* John Knox Press, 1987.

Price, Eugenia. *Getting Through the Night; Finding your way after the loss of a loved one.* Walker & Co., 1985.

Sanford, Doris; Graci Evans. *It Must Hurt a Lot.* Multnomah Press, 1986.

Schiff, Harriett. *Living Through Mourning.* Viking, 1986.

Schuchter, Stephen. *Dimensions of Grief,* Jossey-Bass Publishers, 1986.

Smoke, Jim. *Growing Through Divorce.* Harvest House Publishers, 1986.

_____. *Suddenly Single.* Revell, 1982.

Spiegel, Yorick. *The Grief Process: Analysis and Counselling.* Abingdon, 1977.

Stearns, Ann. *Living Through Personal Crisis.* Ballantine, 1984.

Sullender, R. Scott. *Grief and Growth.* Paulist Press, 1985.

Thielicke, Helmut. *Living With Death.* Eerdmans, 1983.

Viorst, Judith. *Necessary Losses.* Simon & Schuster, 1986.

Wells, Rosemary. *Helping Children Cope With Grief.* Sheldon Press, 1988.

Westburg, Granger. *Good Grief.* Fortress, 1962.

Winter, Richard. *The Roots of Sorrow.* Crossway Books, 1986.

Wylie, Betty Jane. *Survival Guide for Widows.* Ballantine, 1982.

Index

Solitude, time for 13
Spiritual outlook 22
Stearns, Ann Kaiser 106
Steps to recovery 38
Strengthening for grief
  recovery 99
Stress
  diet and 209
  of grief 100
Substance abuse 99
Success 4
Suicide 132, 142
  See also Self-destruction
  children viewing 124, 132
Support community 22
Support group 47, 57, 99,
  143, 146
  for unemployed men 95
  forming a 174
Surgery, reaction to 41
Survival Guide for Widows,
  194
Symptoms of grief 42, 98

T

Talking about grief 13, 22,
  73, 81

Tasks
  grief as a 69
  inability to perform 43, 150
  unpleasant 158
Tears 12, 35, 72, 137
  See also Crying
Time for solitude 13
Time heals 62, 139
Touch, importance of 178
Traditions, family 57
Tranquilizers 16, 28, 52

U

Unresolved grief 96

V

Viewing the body 17, 128

W

Weakness, tears a sign of 72
Why questions 48, 109
Withdrawal 39, 42, 45-46, 51,
  144
Work, going back to 25
Worst kind of grief 65, 67, 77
Wylie, Betty Jane 194